LEARN CREATIVE SCHOOL PROJECTS IN 15 DAYS

(Coding for Arduino)

KRISHNA

ISHAAN

DASHEA

SHARMA

(K.I.D.S)

INDIA • SINGAPORE • MALAYSIA

ISBN 979-8-89133-941-5

Dedicated to our parents

CONTENTS

FOREWORD

We, the K-I-D-S, are delighted at the prospect of bringing out this book for our peers and contemporaries in schools and junior colleges, who feel that their true calling lies in computers and coding; a fact that even their parents recognise. However, they might feel that their imagination is unable to find expression because of the constraints of adequate guidance and seemingly complex coding techniques. We too faced the same problems, till we got around to exploring the world of coding and computers in a simple, easy-to-understand manner. After that, it has been an amazing journey through this new world, where the only thing that has limits is our imagination!

We wanted to share our amazing and innovative journey, which led us to bring out this book for schoolchildren. Trust us; once you get the hang of these simple coding techniques, you can run riot with your imagination and give shape to your fantastic ideas.

I, Krishna, have pursued courses in JAVA, Python and Arduino. I have always been fascinated by technology and like to find technological solutions to common problems.

I, Ishaan, a school student, realized that a huge amount of electricity was being wasted with street lights still glowing, even during the day. I, along with Krishna, rigged up a circuit to switch off lights automatically using Arduino, tested it and both of us were truly elated on finding a simple solution to a problem that we encounter almost daily.

I, Dashea, a school student too, heard different tones being generated using Arduino and a buzzer. We decided to make a testing machine that could be used to assess a patient's hearing. A prototype of a hearing assessment machine was fabricated which we tested on a patient in our family. The thrill that we experienced on seeing it work perfectly cannot be put into words.

These isolated experiences made us think about developing more such projects using Arduino. The coding for these projects is very simple and one need not be an engineer or a senior school student to learn it. Come to think of it, even Ishaan and Dashea (the younger members of our team) found the coding akin to a walk in the park!

Arduino is a palm-sized programmable plastic board on which some electronic components are fitted. It can be used to run and control various equipment by coding it. The coding process itself requires just a few lines of code.

Using this, we started lighting a small LED, running a fan, ringing a doorbell etc., all by writing code running to less than 10 lines. Once these projects were successful, we moved on to some real-world projects and tried our hands at developing them. We got our first adrenaline rush when our programmed Arduino could switch on the security lights of our house when it became dark and switch them off in the morning automatically.

We moved on to a device that could sense the soil humidity in the flowerpots kept in our house and water them automatically as and when they became dry. This proved that we could solve a large number of problems by writing a few lines of code and uploading them onto the Arduino board.

We made a car robot which we controlled from our mobile phone. The robot was made intelligent, and it could sense an obstacle enroute and change its direction. It was as easy as pie!

In this book, we have devoted the first chapter to the common day-to-day problems that we encounter. One page has been intentionally kept blank to allow the reader to spell out the problems that he/she observes and which he/she would eventually like to solve.

The second chapter lists the steps involved in finding a solution to any problem. The next three chapters are devoted to building simple projects which will eventually act as stepping stones towards making bigger projects. Two chapters are devoted to bigger projects like intelligent robots, obstacle-sensing cars, mobile-phone-controlled robots etc.

For the 11th and 12th graders, details of the hardware used in the Arduino board are covered along with the methodology of coding various sensors and actuators.

In writing this book, we have endeavored to share the thrills we experienced while developing our projects. However, this book is just a small drop in the world of coding. The goal is to inspire school children to explore this world for themselves, unleash their talent and use their imagination to create a better world for our own tomorrow. We are certain that all our young readers will gain from this book and enjoy delving into this limitless world!

K.I.D.S

(Krishna, Ishaan, Dashea Sharma)

CONTRIBUTIONS GREATLY ACKNOWLEDGED

At the outset, we acknowledge and express our gratitude to our teachers of Air Force School, Bidar, Kendriya Vidyalaya, Bidar and Army Public School, Dinjan, for their guidance and motivation to work for the society and find solutions to the problems being faced by them.

Our sincere thanks to Mr. Pawan Bharat, Model Institute of Engineering and Technology (Autonomous), Jammu, for his untiring efforts for arranging suitable hardware components for various experiments. He also guided the team on the coding techniques for the Arduino board.

Our parents were a constant source of encouragement and support throughout the process of writing this book. This, and their phenomenal help in editing this book to bring it to its present shape will always be greatly appreciated.

A special mention of Prof. SK Sharma, Model Institute of Engineering and Technology (Autonomous), Jammu, who guided us in conducting experiments and writing codes for the Arduino board.

We greatly acknowledge the contribution of the Arduino company who provided the images and software.

COMMONLY USED TERMS IN ARDUINO/COMPUTERS

Let us set the ball rolling with an explanation of some commonly used terms in computer / coding 'lingo'. We will come across these terms repeatedly in the book and it is worthwhile to get to know these in the beginning itself.

1. **High Level Language (HLL):** This is a computer language in which we write any code (program) for the computer. It contains English-like words like Add, Digital etc. Examples are C, C++, Python, JAVA languages etc.

2. **Machine Language**: It is a language which has only two digits, that are, 0 and 1. All the computers and Arduino understand this language only.

   So, all the programs, written in HLL, have to be converted into the machine language for processing. There is a software, named "compiler", inside the computer which converts the High Level Language to Machine language.

3. **Compiler:** It is a software which converts any high-level language to machine language. Thus, compilers are loaded in all the computers.

   In Arduino, the icon for compiling a code is ✓. Once the Arduino sends a message **'Compiling done',** that means, the code is correctly written as per syntax and has been converted to machine language for use by the Arduino Board.

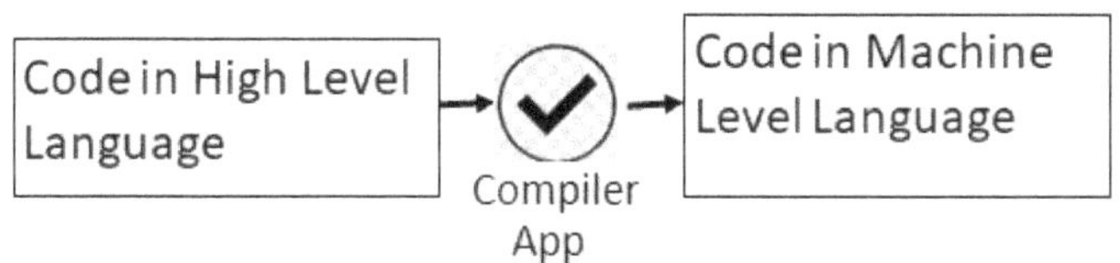

Fig: Conversion of High Level Language to Machine Language using Compiler App

4. **Upload**: It means loading a machine language code, compiled in the computer, onto the Arduino board.
5. **BIT**: It is a short form of **B**inary Dig**it.** In binary mathematics, there are only 2 digits, namely 0 & 1 where as in decimal mathematics there are ten digits namely, 0,1,2, 3…8 and 9. All the computers understand only binary mathematics.
6. **Baud Rate**: A Baud is a measure of speed of data transmission. If one bit is transmitted in one second, then baud rate is 1. In computers, the speed is very high. In Arduino, data is generally transmitted at a speed of 9,600 bits per second. So, baud rate is 9,600.
7. **Ohm:** It is a measure of value of an electronic component called Resistor. Resistors are used for many purposes like restricting current in a device. The value of some of the resistors keeps changing with temperature and light. Such resisters are used as sensors for light and temperature.
8. **Ampere**: It is a unit of current flow in a device. Small currents are measured in milli amperes whereas large currents are measured in amperes.
9. **Various Icons used in Arduino Software**: Once we open the Arduino software, we get the following image. The meaning of each icon is given below the icon.

Compile Upload New Open Save

10. **USB Cable:**It is a cable which connects the computer to other hardware devices like an Arduino Board, printer etc.

    The full form of USB is 'Universal Serial Bus'.
11. **LED**: It is a small light which can glow even when a small voltage of 5 volts is given to it. Its full form is 'Light Emitting Diode'.

Chapter 1

COMMON PROBLEMS; SIMPLE SOLUTIONS!

They say, "All great things begin with asking the right question". We encounter a number of situations in our daily lives that beg for solutions / answers. Wouldn't it be nice if we could find simple solutions to these seemingly tricky problems? How about writing a few lines of code to find automated solutions to these problems? We, the authors identified a few common problems and their solutions, listed below, which we could solve using Arduino and a few simple lines of code.

S.No.	Problem	Solution
1.	**Great Grandpa Feels Warm:** My great-grandfather is bedridden. Everyone in my house goes to work or school and he is alone at home. During summers, when it becomes hot, or the temperature crosses 35^{0}C, he keeps lying on the bed and wishes that someone could switch on a fan or air conditioner for him.	Install a temperature sensor in the room which switches on the fan or air conditioner automatically when the temperature goes beyond 35^{0}C and switches it off once the temperature drops below 30^{0}C. Voila! Great grandpa is happy and comfy!
2.	**Saving Electricity:** The Municipal Committee has fixed streetlights in the streets near my house. Sometimes when I come home at night, I find the street dark as no one has switched on the lights. Also, sometimes in the morning or afternoon, the streetlights are still on because no one has switched them off, thus wasting electricity.	Install a light-detecting sensor which senses the ambient light and switches on the light when it is dark and switches it off when day breaks. Cool, isn't it?
3.	**Watering Plants During Vacations:** While we are on vacation, there is no one in the house to water the indoor and outdoor plants. As a result, some of the plants die by the time we return home after the vacation.	Install a humidity sensor in the pot soil which activates a sprinkler when the soil humidity goes below a certain pre-determined level. No more dead plants when we return!

S.No.	Problem	Solution
4.	**Remote Switching on The House Security Lights:** When we go out in the evening, my father wants someone to switch on our security lights at the main gate, porch and at the rear of the house. Till this is done and confirmed to us, he remains on tenterhooks regarding security of the house.	Install a light-detecting sensor which senses the ambient light and switches on the light when it is dark and switches it off when day breaks. Time to enjoy the evening, Dad!
5.	**Scare of Theft in a Locked House:** When our house is locked and everyone is out; either at school or at work, I sometimes worry about break-ins and robberies.	Install a motion sensor in the house which raises an alarm and gives a ring on your mobile phone that someone has entered the house. Remember the 'Home Alone' movie series? Yes! This is pretty much the same!
6.	**Audiometer for Checking Hearing Acuity** School children need to grasp whatever is being taught in school for effective learning. However, how are they going to do that if their hearing acuity is sub-normal? What if an apparent slow learner actually has impaired hearing? Can we carry out assessment of hearing in school children to catch any hearing impairment early?	Use a tone generator capable of generating tones of different frequencies. This will give us a fair idea of the frequencies at which a child's hearing is impaired. Who knows, the apparent slow learner in class might turn out to be the next Albert Einstein!

FOR THE READER: List The Problems You Encounter and Suggest Solutions		
S.No.	**Problem**	**Suggested Solution**
1.		
2.		
3.		
4.		

Chapter 2

DEVELOPING SOLUTIONS

Ready to roll? Let's start!

We can fabricate a variety of simple projects which can solve common problems, using an Arduino Uno Board. OMG! What on earth is this? Where am I going to find it? Don't start ringing your alarm bells! Arduino Board is a common piece of equipment, easily available in your neighborhood electronics store and easy to understand and configure. Nowadays, the Atal Tinkering Labs in senior secondary schools teach students how to operate this board from 8th or 9th grade. All the projects described in this book have been developed using this board.

What is an Arduino board?

Fig 2.1: Arduino UNO Board

If we remove the cover of a cell phone, we will find a small board, called motherboard, on which a few electronic components are mounted. To make this board function like a mobile phone, a software called Operating System

(OS) is loaded on it. Similarly, when we want to play any game on our phone or tablet, we download the gaming app from the internet, which too gets loaded on the motherboard.

On similar lines, the Arduino board too, is like the mother board of a mobile phone. To make this board functional, an Operating System (OS), known as Integrated Development Environment (IDE) needs to be downloaded from the internet. This IDE makes the board function like a baby computer, ready to be programmed in accordance with our wild imagination.

Is Coding for Arduino Simple?

Coding for this Arduino is very simple. If you want to switch on a light, fan, TV etc. the entire code would be around 5-10 lines only. For example, in case you want to make an LED or a lamp to blink after every one second, then the code will be something like this:

```
void setup()
{  pinMode(9, OUTPUT);  }
void loop()
{  digitalWrite (9, HIGH);
delay(1000);
digitalWrite (9, LOW);
delay(1000);   }
```

Notice that the code runs into merely 7-lines, with a total of 10 words or so. With this code the lamp or LED will keep blinking indefinitely after every one second.

Does the code itself appear complicated? Don't worry! We'll learn more about coding in the subsequent chapters.

Getting Started with Arduino

To use Arduino Board, we need the following items: -

- An Arduino Board
- A computer with a working internet connection
- A USB data cable to connect the Arduino Board to the computer.

A computer is needed to download Arduino IDE from the internet, write code for the project and then upload it on to the Arduino board through a data cable. The initial set up is done as follows: -

1. **Step 1: Download Arduino Software**: On your laptop, download the Arduino software (IDE) from the internet. The icon of this software, as seen on the computer is .

   This software has many programs in it for use. It also compiles the code written by you, i.e., it converts the code to machine language which is easily understood by the Arduino board.

2. **Step 2: Connect Arduino board to the computer** using a USB Cable, as shown in Fig 2.2. It is a special cable with one end like a USB which is inserted in the computer USB port and the second end is compatible with the Arduino Board connector.

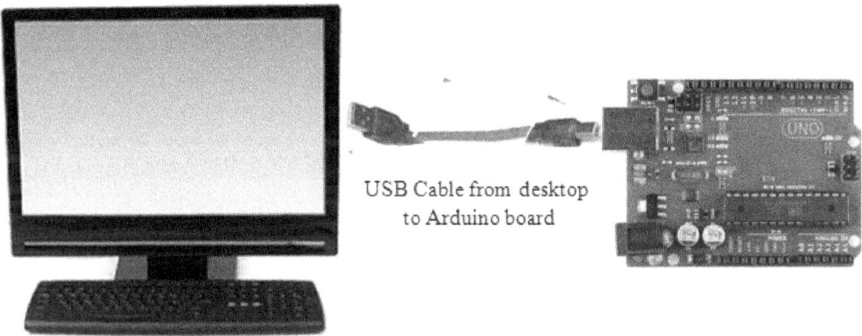

Fig 2.2: Connection between computer and Arduino board

Once connected, the Arduino board starts getting power from the computer. An LED on the board will light up, indicating that it is powered up. The USB cable also helps to upload any code written by us on the computer, on to the Arduino board. Voila! Our Arduino board is now ready to accept any code written on the computer.

3. **Step 3: Check the port of the computer to which the Arduino board is connected:**

   For this, click on the Arduino icon on the computer. If some windows open asking YES or NO, click NO.

   A window, as shown in Fig. 2.3 will appear on the desktop.

   Click **Tools** on the top bar. A new window will open.

   Click **Port**. Note down the number of the port which is displayed on the screen. For example, if it shows "COM7(Arduino UNO)", then that means, the board is connected to Port 7.

   Now if you click on '**COM7 (Arduino Uno**)", then the computer will accept your board as connected and you can use the board now.

File Edit Sketch Tools Help

sketch_jul23a

```
void setup() {
  // put your setup code here, to run once:

}

void loop() {
  // put your main code here, to run repeatedly:

}
```

Fig 2.3: Widow that opens up on clicking Arduino icon on the Computer

   Now if you click "**Tools**" again, a new window opens up showing a menu and against 'Port', it will show **Port: "COM7 (Arduino Uno)"**

4. **Step 4: Check Serviceability of the Arduino Board:** For this, you need to download a sample program of "**Blinking of an LED"** from the basic online libraries available in the software of Arduino. This is done as follows:

   a. On the Arduino program, click **File,** then **Examples,** then **Basics,** then **Blink** (Fig.2.4).

      A program code of "**Blinking an LED**" is seen on the computer (Fig 2.5).

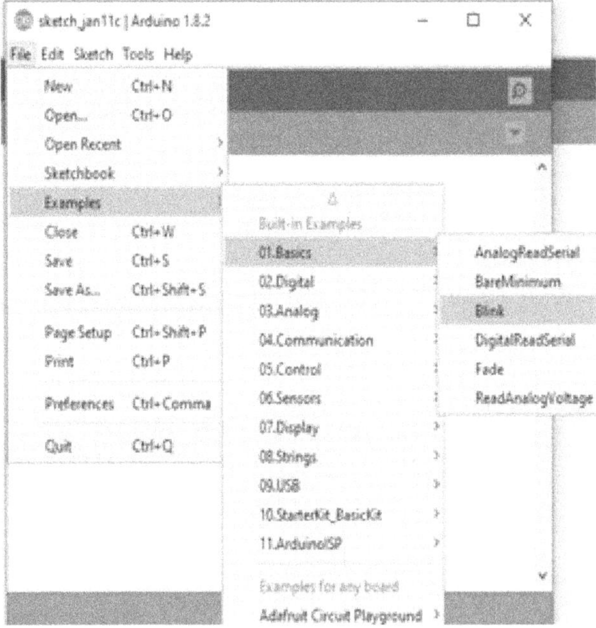

Fig 2.4: Uploading example of "Blinking of and LED from internal libraries"

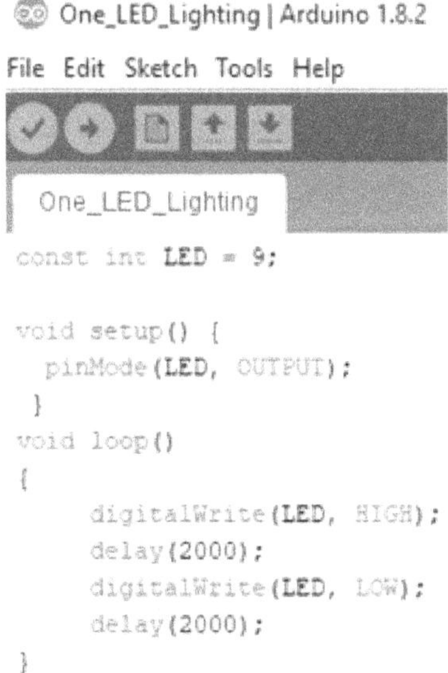


```
const int LED = 9;

void setup() {
  pinMode(LED, OUTPUT);
 }
void loop()
{
     digitalWrite(LED, HIGH);
     delay(2000);
     digitalWrite(LED, LOW);
     delay(2000);
}
```

Fig 2.5: Code for Blinking of an LED

b. **Upload Blinking Code on the Arduino Board**: It is done by clicking on the *'Compile'* icon, followed by the *'Upload'* icon (both of these icons are found below the task bar). This will upload the program from the computer to the Arduino board. At the bottom of the computer screen, you will be able to view sequential messages like *Compiling in Progress, Done Compiling, Uploading in Progress* and finally, *Done Uploading.*

c. Once the program is uploaded, you should be able to see the message **'Done Uploading'.**

d. Now, if the LED on the Arduino board blinks, **that means the Arduino board is serviceable and working** and is ready to accept new codes.

Ready to Build Projects!

Now you are all set to make any project. However, let us start with small projects and learn coding techniques for lighting a lamp, operating a fan, running a motor/wheel of a car and read values of various sensors. Once we are comfortable making these small projects, we will eventually move on to bigger, more complicated ones like mobile-controlled cars, joy-stick controlled robot, smart phone-controlled lights etc.

The first few projects will involve writing small codes of less than 10 lines. Slowly and steadily, we'll build up bigger projects. By the time we finish this book, we should be able to fabricate the following projects:

- Switch on an LED (Light Emitting Diode) and make it blink.
- Make string lights *(lari or jhalar)* of blinking LEDs which are used on occasions like marriages, Diwali etc.
- Use a light sensor to switch on streetlights automatically in the evening and switch them off when day breaks.
- Use a temperature sensor to switch on a fan or air conditioner automatically when it becomes hot.
- Run up to two motors used for making a toy car.
- Detect an obstacle in front of the moving car, stop it and sound a buzzer.
- Make a robotic car and control it from your mobile phone or a joystick or any remote transmitter.

Chapter 3

BLINKING LED

Objectives of this Project

Here, we will learn about a cool piece of electronic equipment called an LED and the code for making it blink. We will eventually learn the following:

- What is an LED?
- How is an LED connected to the Arduino board?
- How the code (called sketch) is written for Arduino?
- Parts of an Arduino code
- Commands used for lighting an LED and the complete code for it to blink.
- Code for 2 blinking LEDs

What is an LED?

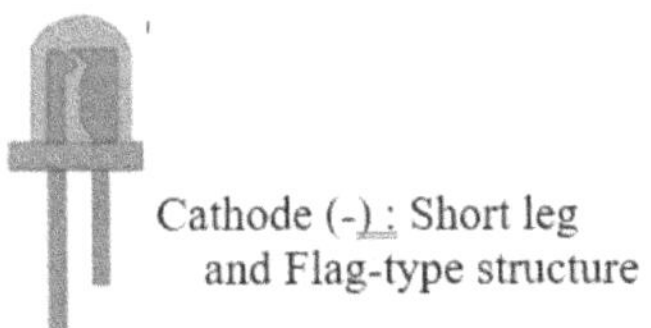

Fig 3.1: Parts of an LED

An LED or a Light Emitting Diode is a device which glows when a little current, say, around 10-20 milliamperes is passed through it. Its length is just around one centimeter and has two terminals called anode and cathode

(Fig.3.1). It emits light when 5 Volts from a battery or cell, is given to its anode and 0 Volt is connected to the cathode.

How does an LED glow?

Small LEDs glow when 5-15 milliamperes (mA) of current is passed through them. It will not glow if the current is less than 5 mA; and if the current is more than 15 mA, it will overheat and stop working.

Fig 3.2: Resistor for LED

When connected to an Arduino board, it draws up to 40 mA, and is likely to overheat and burn. To prevent this from happening, a resistor of around 220 ohms (Fig.3.2) is connected to it.

Making Connections of the Arduino board

One leg of LED (say, Cathode) is connected to one end of the resistor. The other end of the resistor is connected to the 0 Volts (marked as GND, i.e., Ground on the Arduino board). The Anode leg of the LED is connected to any of the 14 digital pins on the Arduino (Fig. 3.3). Refer Chapter 11 for more details of the hardware.

Next, we need to write a code to make it blink. The principle for making this work is that when 5 Volts are passed through the LED, it glows. Next, 0 V is given to it to make it stop glowing. This is repeated with some delay, and we see that the LED blinks.

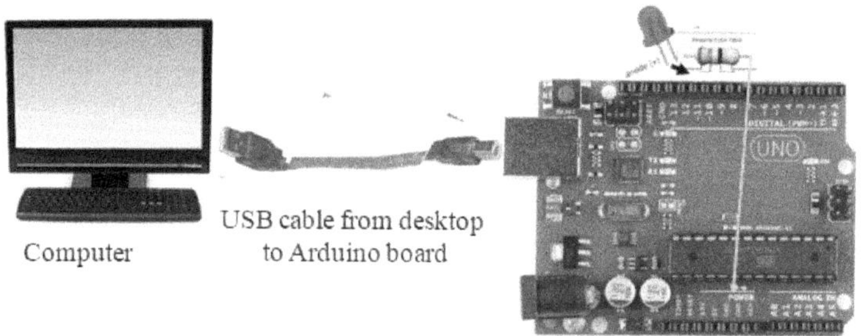

Fig 3.3: Connections of LED & Resistor with Arduino

Writing the Code (Program)

To write the code, we should first know the following:

- What are three 3 blocks or parts in a code and what commands are written in these?
- Common commands used in the code.
- Syntax (grammar) of the code.
- Complete code with meaning of each command. (Screenshots are provided to understand as to how it looks on the computer.)

Parts of Arduino Code:

Arduino Program has 3 parts (or blocks).

- **Part 1:** In the first block, some constants can be declared. For example, if an LED is permanently connected to Pin 9 of Arduino Board, or a temperature sensor is connected to Pin 6, then these are written as:
  const int LED = 9: (*const* stands for constant and *int* for integer e.g. 9)

  const int SENSOR=6;

  After these commands, the words 'LED' and 'SENSOR' (also called variables) will always be understood by Arduino as pins 9 and 6.

- **Part 2:** This part is called **Set Up Block** and written as **void setup( ):** (The inventor of Arduino used the word **void** which means empty or hollow. He made Arduino for beginners whose knowledge is assumed to be hollow about problem solving).

  Under void setup() block, a few statements can be written which are executed by Arduino **only once** e.g., pinMode(9, OUTPUT). This will consider pin 9 of Arduino board as always in Output mode. Items like LED, a fan, an air conditioner, motor etc. can be connected to pin 9.

  Another example is pinMode (8, INPUT). With this command, pin 8 of Arduino will always be considered as Input pin and one can connect sensors or other input devices to it.

- **Part 3:** It is called **Loop Block** and written as **void loop( )**. Here one can write those commands which are to be repeated. An example is a blinking LED which blinks repeatedly, or a motor which is to run continuously.

Some Commands for Arduino: To write any code, one must use many commands. Examples are:

- **digitalWrite (LED, HIGH):** With this command Arduino will generate an output of 5 volts (also written as HIGH) and send to its pin named LED.
- **delay(1000):** This command gives a pause of 1000 milliseconds (1 second). So, if one wants an LED to glow for two seconds then it is written as:

```
digitalWrite(LED, HIGH);
delay(2000);

(Note: the delay ( ) command always processes the time in
milliseconds.)
```

- Any amplification in the code or comment can be written after two slashes //. Example is

```
//This is the first code I am writing
```

Syntax (Grammar) of Arduino:

- All commands are separated by a semicolon (;)
- Setup Block will start and end with curly brackets { }. Same is the case with Loop Block. Examples are:

```
void setup()     { Before all statements, there is a curly
                 bracket and once the  block ends, again one
                 curly bracket } is inserted.
void loop()      { all statements }
```

Complete Code for 'Blinking LED'

Firstly, click on icon of Arduino Software on the computer. A window showing the structure of the code will open on the screen of the computer, as shown in Fig 3.4. In this window, one can delete the code lines written on it and write one's own code.

sketch_jan05a | Arduino 1.8.2

File Edit Sketch Tools Help

sketch_jan05a

```
void setup() {
  // put your setup code here, to run once:

}

void loop() {
  // put your main code here, to run repeatedly:

}
```

Fig 3.4: Widow that opens up on clicking Arduino icon on Computer

Next code is written as shown below. Comments are also inserted for ease of understanding.

1. Under "Declaring Integer Constants", declare Pin 9 as a variable named "LED".

```
Code line is: const int LED = 9;
```

2. Under "void setup", set mode of Pin 9 (LED) as "OUTPUT" only. With this, LED will get +5V when Arduino assigns it HIGH, and it gets 0V when Arduino assigns it LOW.

```
Code line is: pinMode(LED, OUTPUT);
```

3. Under "void loop", write the code for giving 5V to Pin 9, that is, make the pin 9 HIGH.

```
Code line is: digitalWrite (LED,HIGH)
```

4. This code will make LED glow.
5. Now to make it blink, keep it in HIGH mode, for 2 seconds, i.e 2,000 milliseconds. Then make it LOW mode, and again pause for 2 seconds. This will make the LED blink with a gap of 2 seconds.

```
Command for pause is delay(2000)
```

So code lines will be:

```
digitalWrite (LED, HIGH);
delay(2000);
digitalWrite (LED, LOW);
delay(2000);
```

How Does the Code Look on Screen?

Fig 3.5 shows what the code will look like on the computer screen:

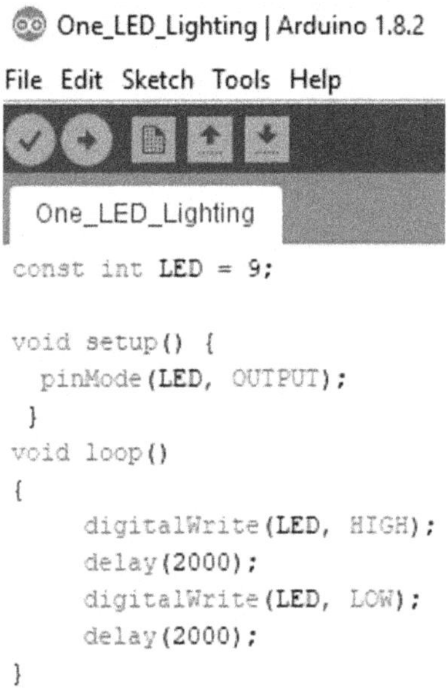

One_LED_Lighting | Arduino 1.8.2

File Edit Sketch Tools Help

One_LED_Lighting

```
const int LED = 9;

void setup() {
  pinMode(LED, OUTPUT);
 }
void loop()
{
      digitalWrite(LED, HIGH);
      delay(2000);
      digitalWrite(LED, LOW);
      delay(2000);
}
```

Fig 3.5: Code for Blinking of LED

Compiling and Uploading Code on Arduino

After writing the code, it is compiled by the computer. For this, click on the 'Compile' icon. If all commands are syntactically (grammatically) correct, i.e. its syntax is correct, a message '**Compiling Done**' starts flashing at the bottom of the computer screen.

Now it can be uploaded onto the Arduino by clicking **Upload** icon.

Once this code is uploaded on to the Arduino board, the LED starts blinking.

Code for Blinking two LEDS

In place of one LED, just connect two LEDS, one at pin 9 and second at PIN 11. Write code as was written earlier.

Sample code is shown in Fig 3.6.

_2_LEDs_Blinking | Arduino 1.8.2

File Edit Sketch Tools Help

_2_LEDs_Blinking

```
const int LED1 = 9;
const int LED2 = 11;
void setup() {
  pinMode(LED1, OUTPUT);
  pinMode(LED2, OUTPUT);
}
void loop() {

      digitalWrite(LED1, HIGH);
      delay(300);
      digitalWrite(LED1, LOW);
      delay(300);
      digitalWrite(LED2, HIGH);
      delay(300);
      digitalWrite(LED2, LOW);
      delay(300);
}
```

Fig 3.6: Code for Blinking of 2 LEDs

Arduino Software

Arduino software, in detail, along with methodology to write codes with examples is written as a separate chapter at the end of this book.

Commands Used in this Chapter

(const int, pinMode, digitalWrite, INPUT, OUTPUT, LOW, HIGH, delay)

1. const int AnyName = 9 <pin No.>
2. pinMode(AnyName, INPUT)
3. pinMode(AnyName, OUTPUT)
4. digitalWrite(AnyName, HIGH)
5. delay(1000)

DIY TIME!

Write a code to make a string light (*lari*) of 5 LEDs, blinking sequentially, one after another repeatedly.

Chapter 4

LIGHT SENSITIVE AUTOMATIC STREET LIGHTS

Need for the Project:

In cities and towns, we often observe that street lights keep glowing even during the day, thus wasting precious electricity. On the contrary, sometimes, when we come home late at night, we find the streets dark since no one remembered to switch them on! Ironic! Isn't it?

So, let us design a project to use Arduino and a light sensor for switching these lights on automatically when it becomes dark and turning these off at dawn.

What will we learn?

In this project, we'll learn about the following:

- A light sensor called LDR and its details.
- Coding for LDR
- Measuring value of LDR and intensity of light with Arduino

What is an LDR Sensor?

The full form of LDR is Light Dependent Resistor. It is a small resistor, the value of which keeps changing with the intensity of light falling on it. A typical LDR will have a resistance of 1000 ohms in the dark and 50 ohms when it is kept in broad daylight.

It is very small in size, maybe 1 cm or so, and has 2 terminals as shown in the figure. LDRs are used as light sensors.

Since the coding for this project will remain largely the same, irrespective of the size of the light (LED or a large street light), in this project, in place of a street light, a simple LED has been used to understand the coding process.

Components Required for the Project

- Arduino UNO board connected to a computer.
- Light sensor LDR.
- Resistor of 10 kilo ohms.
- Jumper wires and breadboard: Needed for connecting sensors, switches etc. to the Arduino board.

Connections with Arduino board

- Connect LDR to a resistor of 10 kilo ohms.
- Connect the junction of LDR and the resister to analog pin A0 of Arduino .
- Connect the other ends of LDR to Vc (+5V) and resistor to 0 V (GND).
- LED: Connect Cathode to Ground and Anode to digital pin 7. An LED is used to depict a streetlight.

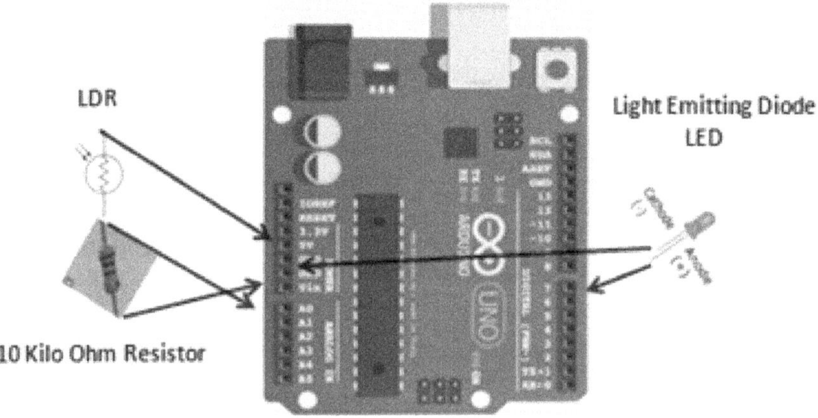

Fig 4.2: Connections of LDR with Arduino

Coding Method:

- In the first part, Digital Pin 11 of Arduino is given the name as **ledPin** and Analog Pin A0 of Arduino is declared as **ldrPin.**
- In the **Set Up Block,** following declarations are done:
  - Declare sensor ldr Pin as **INPUT**
  - Declare led Pin as **OUTPUT**
  - Fix the speed of transfer of data between computer and Arduino as 9,600 baud. (In computer communications, **Baud** is a unit of data speed).
- **In Loop Block,** following actions are taken:
  - Read the value of sensor from ldrPin.
  - If the value is low, i.e., it is dark, then send HIGH (5V) to LED pin to switch it on.
  - Again, if the value is more i.e. it is daylight, then send LOW to LED pin to switch it off.
  - Keep repeating this.
- **Additional Commands Used in this Program**
  - **Serial.begin(9600)** - It sets the speed of data transfer as 9,600 bauds
  - **analogRead(ldrPin) -** It reads the value of LDR resistor in ohms
  - **if ……… else** - This is a loop command. It sets a condition. If this condition is met, then Arduino sends HIGH to LED pin. The condition in this program is if value of resistance is less than 300 ohms.
  - **Serial.println** - In case one wants to see the exact value of the resistance of LDR (based on the light intensity), then this command will print the value of resistance in one line.

Complete Code to Light an LED when it becomes Dark (as sensed by LDR)

```
const int ledPin = 11;
const int ldrPin = A0;
void setup() {
      Serial.begin(9600);
      pinMode(ledPin, OUTPUT);
      pinMode(ldrPin, INPUT);
}
void loop() {
      int ldrStatus = analogRead(ldrPin);
      if (ldrStatus<=300) {
digitalWrite(ledPin, HIGH);
Serial.println("LDR is DARK, LED is ON");
}
      else {
digitalWrite(ledPin, LOW);
Serial.println("--------------");
}
}
```

Code to Read Value of LDRand see it on the computer (serial monitor)

```
void setup ()
      {
      Serial.begin(9600);
      }
void loop()
      {
      int sensorvalue=analogRead(A0);
      Serial.println(sensorvalue);
      delay(1000);
      }
```

Screenshot of Code: Screenshot of code on the screen of the computer is given in Fig. 4.3

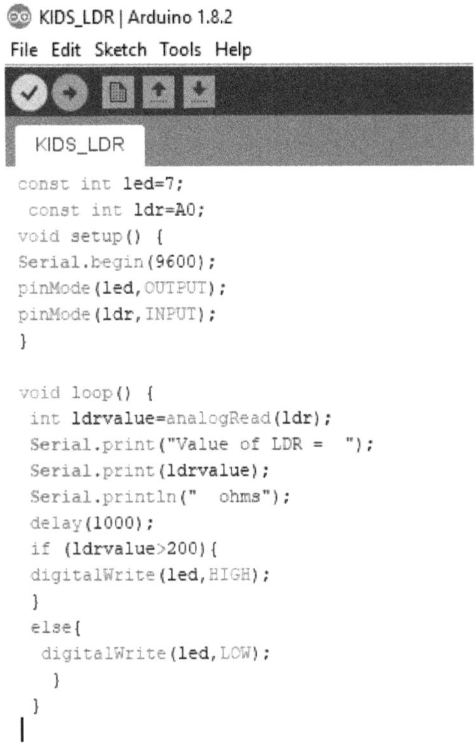

KIDS_LDR | Arduino 1.8.2

File Edit Sketch Tools Help

KIDS_LDR

```
const int led=7;
 const int ldr=A0;
void setup() {
Serial.begin(9600);
pinMode(led,OUTPUT);
pinMode(ldr,INPUT);
}

void loop() {
 int ldrvalue=analogRead(ldr);
 Serial.print("Value of LDR =  ");
 Serial.print(ldrvalue);
 Serial.println("  ohms");
 delay(1000);
 if (ldrvalue>200){
 digitalWrite(led,HIGH);
 }
 else{
  digitalWrite(led,LOW);
   }
 }
```

Fig 4.3: Screenshot of Code for switching on/off a street light and displaying the intensity of light in terms of LDR value

Additional Commands Used in this Chapter

(analogRead, Serial.begin, Serial.print, Serial.println, if..else)

1. analogRead(variable);
2. Serial.begin(9600);
3. Serial.print("Prints whatever is within quotes ");
4. Serial.println("Prints whatever is within quotes"), and go to the next line
5. if …. else command

   If (Condition is met do AAA), else(do BBB)

FUN TIME!

In place of using an LDR and a resistor, use an LDR Module, as shown.

LDR Module is a combination of an LDR and a resistor and hence easy to use.

Use it with Arduino Board and see the fun.

Chapter 5

TEMPERATURE SENSING SWITCH FOR FAN & A/C

Need for the Project:

The legendary Indian summer heat can make life pretty miserable; more so for bedridden patients and old people who would probably find it challenging to get up, reach out for the switchboard and switch on an electric appliance like a fan or air conditioner. Wouldn't it be cool if these appliances could be switched on automatically once the temperature went beyond a certain level and switched off once it dropped below that level? Let's try our hands at one such device!

What will we learn?

In this project, we'll learn about the following:

- Temperature sensor DHT-11
- Coding for a temperature sensor
- Coding for display of room temperature on the screen

What is a Temperature Sensor?

A temperature sensor is a small device which measures the temperature or heat of an object or body. In effect, it is actually like the thermometer that we use to measure our body temperature whenever we fall sick. However, the sensors which we are going to use in this project need to be compatible with Arduino. These are DHT-11 and DHT-22.

DHT is Digital Humidity and Temperature. Hence, as the name suggests, this sensor measures both the temperature and humidity and gives a digital output.

What does DHT-11 look like?

A DHT-11 has 3 pins (Fig 5.1). Two pins are connected to the power supply i.e. 5V and 0V (GND) of Arduino Board. We get the value of temperature as well as humidity from the 3rd pin.

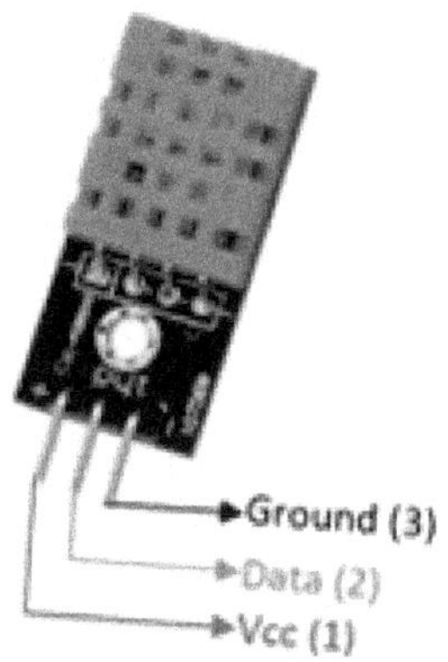

Fig. 5.1: Temperature Sensor DHT-11

Which DHT-11should we use?

Many companies manufacture DHT-11. One, which is compatible with Arduino, is manufactured by Adafruit Industries. The software/app to use DHT with Arduino is available in the *Library* and can also be downloaded from the internet. The complete code of DHT-11 is also available in this library.

Downloading codes of *DHT11 Adafruit* and *DHT11 Unified Sensor* from the Internet

We start by downloading the code for DHT11 from the internet. For this, the computer should be connected to the internet. Procedure for downloading the code is as under:

1. Open the Arduino software by clicking on Arduino icon.
2. Click on **Sketch>Include Library>Manage Libraries>**

   (wait for 30-40 seconds for the libraries to get downloaded from the internet)

3. A window will open showing all the programs in the library. We have to download DHT11 of Adafruit model. For this, in the search bar with 3 fields, we notice that, two fields are already filled and the third is empty. Filled fields are 'Type = **All**' and 'Topic=**All**'. Wait till the libraries get downloaded from the internet.

4. Bring the cursor on the third field and type **DHT.** A library of all DHT codes written by various companies and accepted by Arduino will be shown. We need to download the code written by Adafruit Company. So, look for **DHT by Adafruit**.

5. When we see **DHT11 by Adafruit** in the libraries, click on *More Info* (written at the bottom). The version of this code is also seen. Now click on *Install.* When it gets installed, we see the message '*Installed*' in light green colour, in front of the DHT11 Adafruit program.

   This will now always be available on your computer hard disc/ C drive or documents.

6. Now similarly, also download **Adafruit Unified Sensor**. It is available at the bottom of the programs in the library. Click on *More Info*; and then *Install.* Again, when it gets installed, its colour becomes green (installed).

7. Program of DHT11, downloaded from the internet, should be included in the Sketch as under:

   - Open Arduino software on the computer. Click **File**. Delete the existing sketch and copy the downloaded program.
   - Click **File>Save As** *DHT Program* (give any name to it). Now this program is saved in the sketchbook of the software.

After saving, compile it by clicking the '*Compile*' icon.

Before uploading this compiled program onto the Arduino board, make suitable connections on the Arduino board.

Once the libraries are downloaded, then the DHT program of the library is stored in the File. It can be accessed as under:

File > Examples > (At the bottom of all examples, we can see **"Examples from Custom Libraries".** Under this we find 2 folders, named

"Adafruit BMP085 Unified" and **"TinyDHT Sensor Library".** By clicking **TinyDHT Library,** we can open the code of DHT, as supplied by the Adafruit. This code can be used directly or can be copied in **File > New** >and saved as your own program.

Hardware Connections on the Board

Make hardware connections of DHT and Fan as shown in Fig. 5.2.

- **DHT 11**: Connect one pin to Ground (0 Volts), second pin (Vcc) to +5V. Connect its output pin to pin 7 (or any digital pin) on the board.
- **Fan**: Connect one wire of fan to Ground and second output wire to pin 9 (or any other pin) on the board

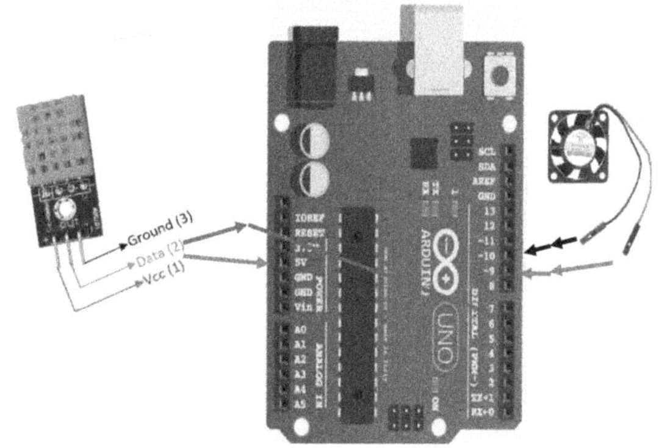

Fig. 5.2: Connection of DHT-11 and Fan with Arduino

Initial Actions for the Project

1. Prepare the Arduino board and check its serviceability.
2. Download DHT11 Adafruit code from the internet. Next download DHT11 unified.
3. Make the (write) code for DHT11.
4. Compile the code.
5. Upload the code onto the Arduino board. Rub DHT11 with your hand to make its temperature go above 35^0C and see the results.

6. Do one more fun activity: See the value of temperature and humidity on the serial monitor of the desktop.
7. Have additional fun. Change value of temperatures in the code written, compile it, upload, and see the efficacy.

Additional Commands in the Program

While writing program, following additional commands will be required:

- **In Part 1:**

```
#include "DHT.h"  -  This includes a library named DHT.h
#define DHTPIN 7 - Defines pin 7 as DHTPIN
#define DHTTYPE DHT11 -  From the library, pick up DHT11 for use.
```

There could be other DHTs also like DHT22 etc.

```
DHT dht(DHTPIN, DHTTYPE)-  From DHTTYPE as DHT11, pick up data
from pin 7(DHTPIN)
```

- **In Set Up Block:**

```
dht.begin() - the program of dht, downloaded earlier, starts
float h = dht.readHumidity()   - Read humidity
float t = dht.readTemperature()- Read temperature as Centigrade
float f = dht.readTemperature(true)-  Read temperature as
Fahrenheit
```

- **In LoopBlock:**

```
Serial.print- Prints value on the computer
Serialprintln- Prints value on computer and goes to start of
the next line
```

Complete Code

```
#include "DHT.h"     //This includes a library named DHT.h
#define DHTPIN 7     // Defines pin 7 as DHTPIN

#define DHTTYPE DHT11  //From the library, pick up DHT11 for use.
                     //There could be other DHTs also like DHT22
                       etc.
DHT dht(DHTPIN, DHTTYPE);    //From DHTTYPE as DHT11, pick up data
                             // from pin 7(DHTPIN)
const int REDLED = 9;        // Dedicated Pin 9 for REDLED

void setup() {
pinMode(REDLED, OUTPUT);  // Declare pin 9 (REDLED) as OUTPUT pin
dht.begin();
digitalWrite(REDLED,LOW);   // Initially, turn off the LED.
Serial.println("Temperature and Humidity Data");  // Print a
message on the Monitor
Serial.begin(9600); // Keep the communication speed between Arduino
                    // and Computer as 9600 bauds
}
void loop() {
      delay(500);
      // set the cursor to column 0, line 1
      // (note: line 1 is the second row, since counting begins with 0):

float h = dht.readHumidity();    // read humidity
float t = dht.readTemperature(); // Read temperature as Centigrade
float f = dht.readTemperature(true);  // Read temperature as
Fahrenheit

if (isnan(h) || isnan(t) || isnan(f)) {
      //lcd.print("ERROR");
return;  // isnan means "Is Not A Number"
      // In Floating Pt, if we get some character other than a number,
then print ERROR
  }
Serial.print(F("Humidity: "));
Serial.print(h);
Serial.print(F("% ;  Temperature: "));
Serial.print(t);
Serial.print(F("°C OR  "));
Serial.print(f);
```

```
Serial.println(F("  degrees F"));

 if(t>26){// See if the temperature is more than 26°C
digitalWrite(REDLED, HIGH);    // The yellow led will turn on.
  }
 else if(t<22){ // If the temperature is lower than 22°C.
digitalWrite(REDLED, LOW);      // The blue led will turn on.
   }
}
```

Upload DHT Program on to the Arduino Board and see the result

From the sketchbook, open DHT 11 program. To upload it onto the Arduino Board, click the *Upload* icon.

Note:

a. Arduino board can hold only one program at one time. So, if you upload this program of DHT, it will stay on the board till you upload another program, thereby erasing the first one.

b. Note that in the DHT program, FAN is connected to pin 9 and DHT output to pin 7 and Temperature is set to 30^{0}C.

Rub the DHT with your hand to increase the temperature of the sensor. We'll see that when temperature is >26^{0}C, the fan will run and when the temperature drops below 22^{0}C, it stops.

Have one more Fun: Change the temperature

- Open the DHT Program
- Change the temperature at which fan should operate to 36^{0}C.
- Now compile this program and upload on to the board.
- You see that the fan will operate only when the temperature is above 36^{0}C.

Have Additional Fun: See the value of Temperature and Humidity on the Serial Monitor

- Open DHT program
- Include following commands:

```
// Print a message to the Monitor of computer.
Serial.println("Temperature and Humidity Data");
Serial.begin(9600);
}

void loop() {
delay(1000);
  // set the cursor to column 0, line 1
  // (note: line 1 is the second row, since counting begins with 0):
  // read humidity
  float h = dht.readHumidity();
   float t = dht.readTemperature();
  // Read temperature as Fahrenheit
  float f = dht.readTemperature(true);

  if (isnan(h) || isnan(t) || isnan(f)) {
    //lcd.print("ERROR");
return;
  }
Serial.print(F("Humidity: "));
Serial.print(h);
Serial.print(F("%  Temperature: "));
Serial.print(t);
Serial.print(F("°C "));
Serial.println(f);
```

- Once we run the program, we see the value of temperature and humidity after each second being written on the monitor.

Let's apply this Knowledge

Write a code to measure temperature and humidity of soil in a flowerpot (*gamla*). Connect a sprinkler to the out pin of Arduino board in place of fan. When temperature becomes high and soil is dry, start the sprinkler to make the soil wet and see the fun!

Chapter 6

CONTROLLING HOME APPLIANCES WORKING ON 230 V AC MAINS

Need

In our houses we have appliances like tube lights, fans, televisions, refrigerators, washing machines etc. These work on 230 V AC. However, the experiments we are performing with Arduino need 5V DC for its functioning. It drives items like LEDs, fans which work on 5 V DC etc.

Hence, can we use a device which will help us to operate our home appliances working on 230 V AC. This device is called a Relay.

What will we learn?

In this project, we'll learn about the following:

- Functioning of a relay
- Connection of relay with switches at our residences working on 230 V AC

What is a Relay?

A relay is a device which takes 5 V DC as its input and can connect any appliance to 230 V AC. One such relay, in a module form, is shown at Fig. 6.1

Fig 6.1: 5V Relay

Functioning of Relay Module

Relay module has 3 pins (A, B and C) on one side and three connections (NC, COM, NO) on the other side. This module is activated by giving 5 V and 0 V (GND) at its pins A and B from the Arduino Board. Third pin C gets input from the digital pin of the Arduino Board.

On the other side, one connection (COM) is connected to the 230 V AC. And the second connection (NC) is connected to the home appliance.

When we write a code HIGH at its input pin C, an internal coil, inside the relay module, gets magnetized and makes the connection of COM (230 V AC) to the other connection NC. So, 230 V is extended to the bulb which is connected as shown in Fig. 6.2.

Connections of Relay with Arduino

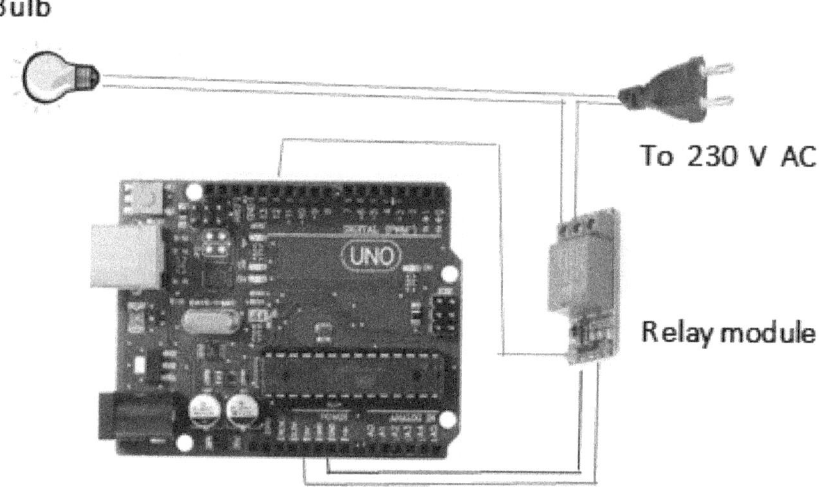

Fig 6.2: Connection of Relay Module and Arduino

Let's apply this Knowledge

Connect an LDR module to one of the input pins of Arduino board. On the output pin, connect a relay and a bulb.

Write a code to sense the light intensity (from LDR module) and switch on a 230 V bulb when the light intensity becomes low (that is, it gets dark) and vice versa.

Chapter 7

DETECTING AN OBSTACLE AND SOUNDING A BUZZER

Need of the Project:

Visually impaired people can do with a smart stick for walking which can sense an obstacle and sound an alarm for the user so that he/she can change the route. A similar situation can arise in a car being driven by a drowsy or inattentive person.

An obstacle sensor which senses the obstacle and sounds a buzzer to alert the user / driver would be an ideal solution to this problem.

Besides this, a buzzer can be used to check the hearing (auditory) acuity of students or hearing-impaired persons. Buzzers can generate sounds of various frequencies. Hence, the hearing loss at various frequencies can be ascertained. Let us stretch our imagination a little further. If we could control the volume output of the buzzer and quantify the volume (in dB), we could have a working audiometer on our hands! However, let us not get too ahead of ourselves. Simple things first!

What will we learn?

In this project, we'll learn details of the following:

- An IR proximity sensor module to sense obstacle
- A buzzer module and the tones it can generate.
- Coding of IR sensor and buzzer for Arduino

What is an IR Proximity Sensor Module?

IR stands for Infra-Red wave. This wave, once transmitted in air, moves in a straight line and gets reflected when some obstacle comes in front of it.

IR Proximity Sensor has got two LEDs. One LED acts as a transmitter and the second one as a receiver. (Fig. 7.1)

When switched on, the transmitter LED transmits IR wave. If some obstacle comes in its route, it gets reflected and is received by the receiver LED. It gives a signal at its data pin.

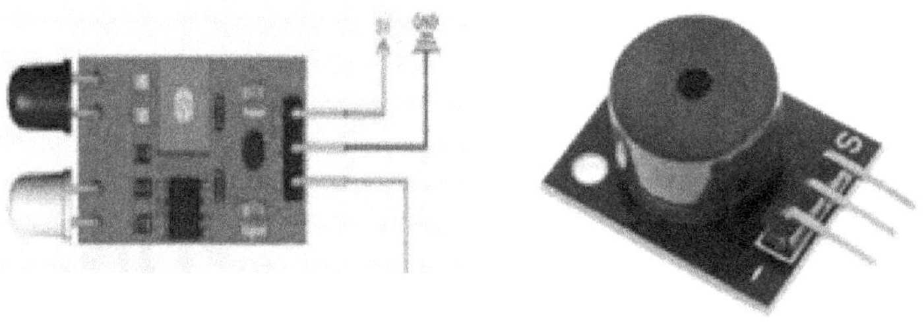

Fig 7.1: IR Sensor Module and Buzzer

This module has 3 pins. Two pins are connected to 5V and GND of Arduino whereas the third pin is a Data pin on which the signal or 5V is received once an obstacle is encountered enroute.

Buzzer and its Details

The buzzer is a small component, which when connected to 5V and GND of Arduino, generates tones. Frequency of tones can be changed by writing value of frequency in code.

Connections

One leg of both the IR Sensor and buzzer is connected to 5V of Arduino and second leg to GND. Data pin of IR module is connected to a pin which is made as INPUT pin whereas the third pin of the buzzer is declared as OUTPUT pin.

Once these devices get 5V from Arduino, these become active.

Additional Commands Used for Buzzer

There are two commands used for buzzer and these are:

- **tone(buzzer,** ***frequency*****)**
- **noTone(buzzer)**

If the code line is written as **tone(buzzer, 50)** then buzzer will generate a tone of 50 hertz. And if it is written as **tone(buzzer, 200)** then the tone generated will be of 200 hertz frequency.

When code line **noTone(buzzer)** is noticed, then the buzzer will stop giving any sound.

Code for Buzzer to Generate sound of frequency 50 hertz

Code of beeping tone after every one second is shown in Fig 7.2.

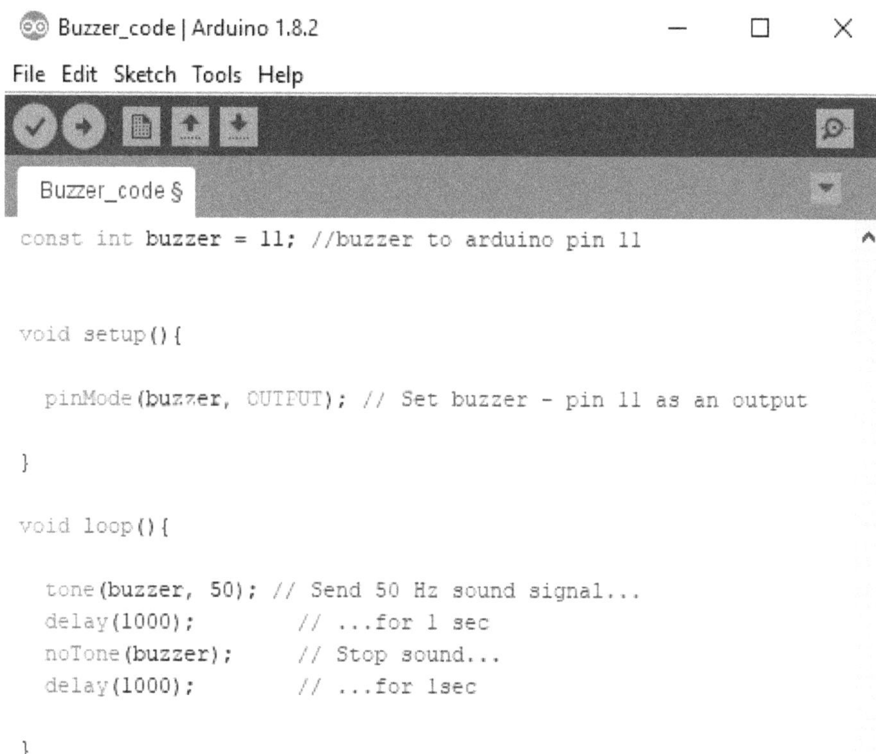


```
const int buzzer = 11; //buzzer to arduino pin 11


void setup(){

  pinMode(buzzer, OUTPUT); // Set buzzer - pin 11 as an output

}

void loop(){

  tone(buzzer, 50); // Send 50 Hz sound signal...
  delay(1000);        // ...for 1 sec
  noTone(buzzer);     // Stop sound...
  delay(1000);        // ...for 1sec

}
```

Fig 7.2: Screenshot of Code written for Buzzer with tone of 50 Hertz

Code for Generating tone on Seeing an Obstacle

Screenshot of the code written for generating a tone of 100 hertz after every one second, on seeing the obstacle is given at Fig. 7.3.

IR_sounds_Buzzer_Testing | Arduino 1.8.2

File Edit Sketch Tools Help

IR_sounds_Buzzer_Testing

```
int SensorPin = 8;
int BuzzerPin = 11;

void setup() {
  pinMode(BuzzerPin, OUTPUT);
  pinMode(SensorPin, INPUT);
  Serial.begin(9600);
}

void loop() {
  int SensorValue = digitalRead(SensorPin);
   if (SensorValue==LOW){ // LOW MEANS Object Detected
    tone(BuzzerPin, 100); // Send 50 Hz sound signal...
  delay(1000);          // ...for 1 sec
  noTone(BuzzerPin);       // Stop sound...
  delay(1000);          // ...for 1sec
  }
  else
  {
    digitalWrite(BuzzerPin, LOW);
  }
}
```

Fig. 7.3: Screenshot of Code written for Buzzer and IR Sensor

Application of Buzzer

Make an Ear-testing Machine

Write a code to generate tones of 50 Hz, 100 Hz, 200, Hz …… 10,000 Hz. Each tone should sound for 5 seconds, one after another.

Now check whether you can hear all the tones. (*The hearing impaired will not be able to hear all the tones.*)

Chapter 8

ROBOTIC CAR

General

In this chapter, we will endeavour to learn coding of motors so that one can make an auto-rickshaw or car, move it forward, backward, right or left and also stop it when some obstacle is encountered.

Items Needed

1. **Wheels:** These are normal wheels used in the toy cars
2. **DC Motors (Gear type):** The wheels are fixed to the shaft of the motors. DC motors are used for this purpose. These run when 5 volts are applied to them. Speed of motor shaft is around 100 RPM (Revolutions Per Minute), which is very high for tyres. So, to reduce the speed, we use gears or use Gear Motors only. Gear motors run at 5-12 Volts DC. They take a minimum of 100 milliamperes of current. If we have to run these motors with the help of Arduino, then a Current Driver too is required.

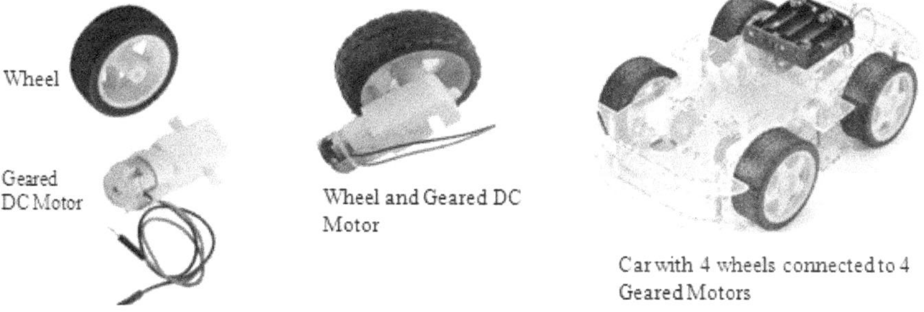

Fig 8.1: Wheels and Geared DC Motors in a toy car

3. **Current Driver for Motors:** Arduino pins usually gives up to 40 milliamperes of current at each of their pins. To run a motor, one needs at least 100 milliamperes of current. So, a current driver is needed.

4. **Current Driver IC LN293D**: It can give 3 to 35 volts and 2 amperes of current. So, it can be used to drive two motors for toy cars to move these in forward as well as reverse directions.

Details of Current Driver and Pin Connection Diagram:

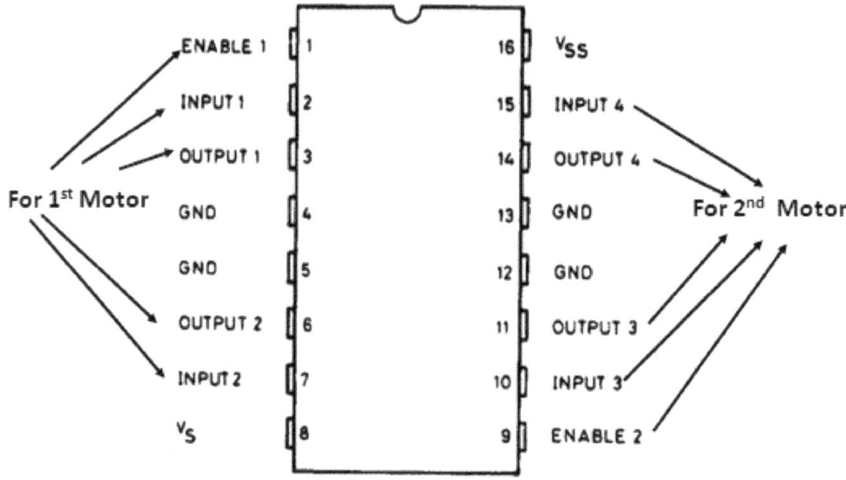

Fig 8.2: Pin Connections of IC LN293 D (Current Driver)

It is an IC (integrated circuit) which can run 2 motors at one time. Pins on the left side are numbered from 1 to 8 and are used for running motor no. 1. On the right side, we have pin numbers 9 to 16 which are used to run motor no. 2. Details of pin layout are as under:

- Pin 8 – It is the Vs pin and is connected to Vc of Arduino where 5V DC is always available. Driver gets 5 V at this pin from Arduino.
- Pins 4, 5, 12 and 13 – These are Ground pins (GND) and are connected to GND of Arduino (means 0 volts).
- Pin 1 – ENABLE 1- When this pin gets 5 V, it enables all pins for Motor 1. So, to start Motor 1, this pin should be given 5V (Or made HIGH)

- Pins 2 and 7: These are INPUT for motor 1 pins and the driver get inputs (5V or 0V called HIGH or LOW) from Arduino based on the code.
- Pins 3 & 6: These are OUTPUT pins. Once the driver gets inputs at pins 2 & 7, it amplifies the current and makes it available at pins 3 & 6 to which the motors are connected.

Similarly, there are pins 9,10,11,14, 15 and 16 for Motor 2.

Movement Directions of Motors:

Motors go forward or backward depending on the voltage at their pins.

For Motor 1:

Clockwise (Forward) Direction: Give HIGH to Pin 2 and LOW to Pin 6

Counter clockwise (Reverse) direction: Give LOW to Pin 2 and HIGH to Pin 6

Truth Table for **First motor** is:

Enable Pin 1 (2 for 2nd motor)	Output Pin 2 (10 for 2nd motor)	Output Pin 7 (15 for 2nd motor)	Motor's Rotation
HIGH	HIGH	LOW	Clockwise
HIGH	LOW	HIGH	Anti clockwise
Any	HIGH	HIGH	No rotation
Any	LOW	LOW	No rotation

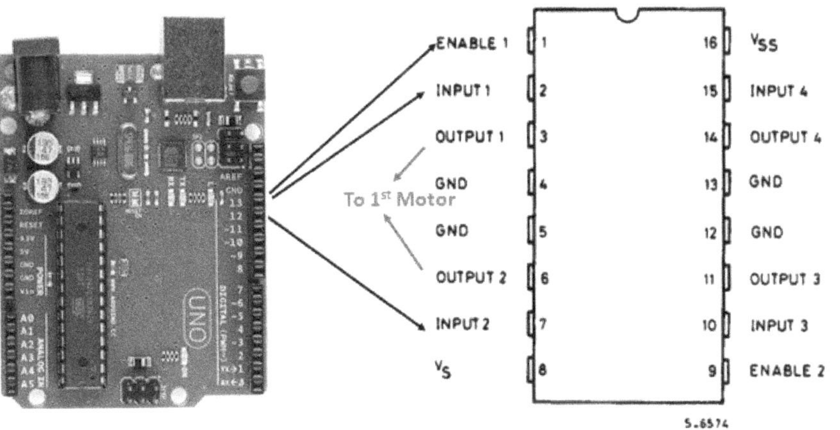

Fig 8.3: Connections among Arduino, Current Driver and 1st Motor

Code to Drive an Auto Rickshaw

```
//Pins of Motor A
const int motorPin1  =7;  // Pin 10 of L293
const int motorPin2  =5;  // Pin 15 of L293

//Pins of Motor B
const int motorPin3  =9; // Pin 7 of L293
const int motorPin4  = 11;  // Pin 2 of L293

void setup(){

//Set pins as outputs
pinMode(motorPin1, OUTPUT);
pinMode(motorPin2, OUTPUT);
pinMode(motorPin3, OUTPUT);
pinMode(motorPin4, OUTPUT);

// motorPin1 and motorpin2 are for Motor A:
// motorpin3 and motorpin4 are for Motor B:

//This code will turn Motor A counter-clockwise for 2 sec.
digitalWrite(motorPin1, LOW);
digitalWrite(motorPin2, HIGH);
digitalWrite(motorPin3, LOW);
digitalWrite(motorPin4, HIGH);
delay(1000);

//This code will turn Motor B clockwise for 2 sec.
digitalWrite(motorPin1, HIGH);
digitalWrite(motorPin2, LOW);
digitalWrite(motorPin3, HIGH);
digitalWrite(motorPin4, LOW);
delay(1000);

//This code will turn Motor B counter-clockwise for 2 sec.
digitalWrite(motorPin1, LOW);
digitalWrite(motorPin2, LOW);
digitalWrite(motorPin3, LOW);
digitalWrite(motorPin4, HIGH);
delay(1000);
```

```
//And this code will stop motors
digitalWrite(motorPin1, LOW);
digitalWrite(motorPin2, HIGH);
digitalWrite(motorPin3, LOW);
digitalWrite(motorPin4, LOW);
delay(1000);

digitalWrite(motorPin1, LOW);
digitalWrite(motorPin2, LOW);
digitalWrite(motorPin3, LOW);
digitalWrite(motorPin4, LOW);
}
void loop()
{
}
```

Screenshot of Code for moving 2 motors using Current Driver

In the screenshot given at Fig. 8.4, code is written for moving 2 motors using a current driver. These motors move in a forward direction for 2 seconds, stop for 1 second, move in reverse direction for another 2 seconds and finally stop for 1 second. This cycle is repeated endlessly.

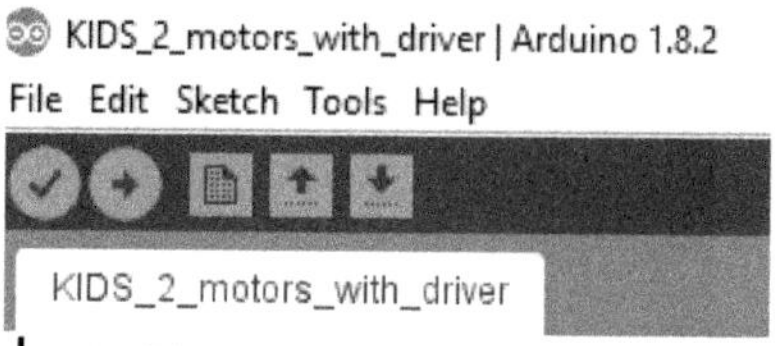

KIDS_2_motors_with_driver | Arduino 1.8.2

File Edit Sketch Tools Help

KIDS_2_motors_with_driver

```
// Pins of Motor A
const int motorPin1=7;
const int motorPin2=5;

// Pins of Motor B
const int motorPin3=9;
const int motorPin4=11;
void setup() {
   pinMode(motorPin1, OUTPUT);
   pinMode(motorPin2, OUTPUT);
   pinMode(motorPin3, OUTPUT);
   pinMode(motorPin4, OUTPUT);
 }
void loop() {
  digitalWrite(motorPin1,HIGH);
  digitalWrite(motorPin2, LOW);
  digitalWrite(motorPin3,HIGH);
  digitalWrite(motorPin4, LOW);
  delay(2000);

  digitalWrite(motorPin1,LOW);
  digitalWrite(motorPin2, LOW);
  digitalWrite(motorPin3,LOW);
  digitalWrite(motorPin4, LOW);
  delay(1000);

  digitalWrite(motorPin1,LOW);
  digitalWrite(motorPin2, HIGH);
  digitalWrite(motorPin3,LOW);
  digitalWrite(motorPin4, HIGH);
  delay(2000);

 digitalWrite(motorPin1,LOW);
 digitalWrite(motorPin2, HIGH);
 digitalWrite(motorPin3,LOW);
 digitalWrite(motorPin4, HIGH);
 delay(2000);

 digitalWrite(motorPin1,LOW);
 digitalWrite(motorPin2, LOW);
 digitalWrite(motorPin3,LOW);
 digitalWrite(motorPin4, LOW);
 delay(1000);
}
```

Fig. 8.4: Screenshot of 2 motors moving in forward and reverse directions

Application

Write a code to move a car on a preset path as shown.

Chapter 9

CONTROLLING A CAR REMOTELY USING A MOBILE PHONE

(USE OF BLUETOOTH MODULE)

Need

Wouldn't it be cool to control a variety of devices remotely and that too from one's mobile phone. This can be easily achieved in Arduino by using just a simple Bluetooth module.

What is a Bluetooth Module?

It is a small single-chip board, of around 2x1 inches size. It acts as a simple communication channel between a mobile phone and Arduino. Whatever commands we give from our mobile phone, it understands and transmits to Arduino. This way, we can control any device remotely.

There are a number of Bluetooth modules available in the market. However, the common ones are HC-06, HC-05 and HM-10.

Bluetooth Module HC-06

This module has 4 pins (two for Power – Vcc and GND & 2 for receiving and transmitting data). To use this, connect Vcc with 5V of Arduino and GND with GND of Arduino.

Rx and Tx pins are the Receive and Transfer pins respectively. The module receives the serial data from the mobile phone through Rx pin and then transfers that data to the Arduino using its Tx pin.

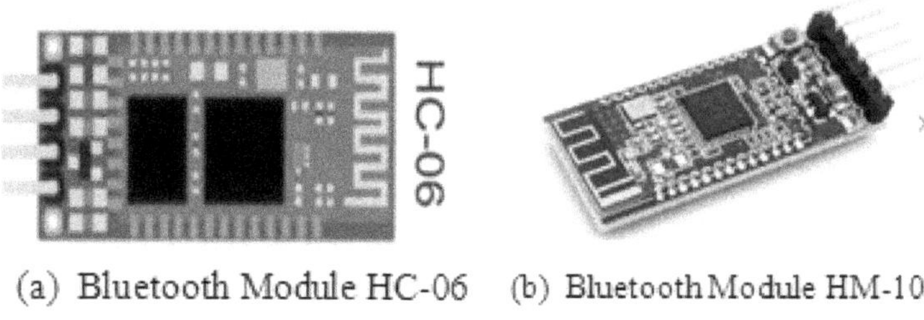

Fig 9.1: Bluetooth Modules HC-06 and HM-10

The Tx pin on the module is connected directly to the Rx pin on the Arduino whereas the Rx pin on the module is connected to the Tx pin on the Arduino. Use of Tx pin of module also helps in generating 3.3V which is needed by the Bluetooth module. Connections of Arduino and Bluetooth module pins are as shown in the figure 9.2.

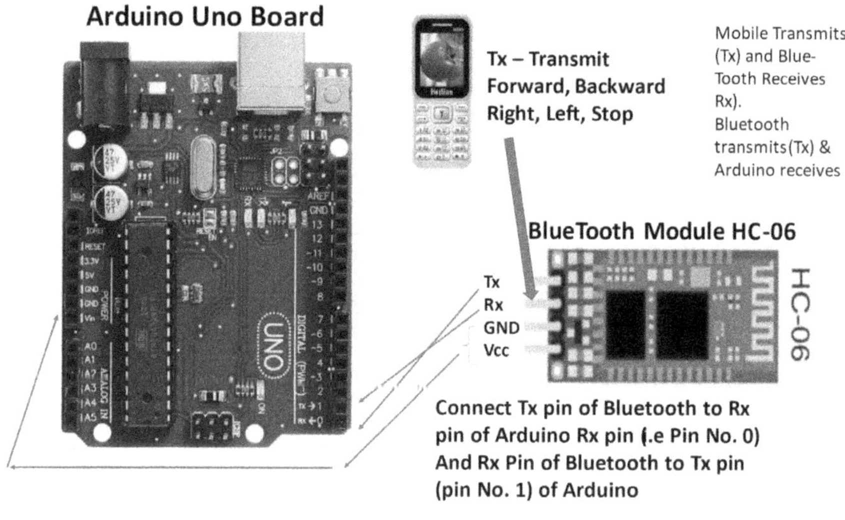

Fig 9.2: Connections between Arduino board and HC-06

Bluetooth Module HM-10

Another Bluetooth module commonly used is HM-10 (Fig. 9.1(b)). It is also very easy to use. In the projects described here, any one of these modules can be used depending upon availability.

Configuring mobile phone to control direction of motors remotely

For using Bluetooth module, the mobile phone needs to be configured, so that it has the icons to move the motors in the forward, reverse, right and left directions and an icon for stopping it.

Bluetooth module generally has a password or PIN to operate. In case of HC-06, it is 1234 by default.

To pair it with a mobile phone, turn on Bluetooth on it and search for neighboring active devices. One of the active devices seen on the mobile screen will be HC-06. Pair this device.

Code for Controlling Direction of Motors remotely

A sample code for moving two motors in different directions is written below. It can be tried by students and tested.

```
#include <SoftwareSerial.h>
SoftwareSerialBluetooth(2, 3);          // (TXD, RXD) of HM-10
char BT_input;                          // to store input character
received via BT.
int motorPin1 = 7;                      // pin 2 on L293D IC
int motorPin2 = 5;                      // pin 7 on L293D IC
int motorPin3 = 9;                     // pin 15 on L293D IC
int motorPin4 = 11;                     // pin 10 on L293D IC

void setup()
{
Bluetooth.begin(9600);
Serial.begin(9600);
pinMode(motorPin1, OUTPUT);
pinMode(motorPin2, OUTPUT);
pinMode(motorPin3, OUTPUT);
pinMode(motorPin4, OUTPUT);
}

void loop()
{
  if (Bluetooth.available())
  {
```

```
BT_input=Bluetooth.read();
    if (BT_input=='s')
    {
digitalWrite(motorPin1, LOW);
digitalWrite(motorPin2, LOW);
digitalWrite(motorPin3, LOW);
digitalWrite(motorPin4, LOW);
Serial.println("Motors are Off");
    }
    else if (BT_input=='b')
    {
digitalWrite(motorPin1, LOW);
digitalWrite(motorPin2, HIGH);
digitalWrite(motorPin3, LOW);
digitalWrite(motorPin4, HIGH);
Serial.println("Motors are rotating left");
    }
    else if (BT_input=='f')
    {
digitalWrite(motorPin1, HIGH);
digitalWrite(motorPin2, LOW);
digitalWrite(motorPin3, HIGH); digitalWrite(motorPin4, LOW);
Serial.println("Motors are rotating right");
    }
   else if (BT_input=='r')
    {
digitalWrite(motorPin1, HIGH);
digitalWrite(motorPin2, LOW);
digitalWrite(motorPin3, LOW);
digitalWrite(motorPin4, HIGH);
Serial.println("First Motor is rotating right & Second is left");
    }
    else if (BT_input=='l')
    {
digitalWrite(motorPin1, LOW);
digitalWrite(motorPin2, HIGH);
digitalWrite(motorPin3, HIGH);
digitalWrite(motorPin4, LOW);
Serial.println("First Motor is rotating Left & second is right");
    }
  }
}
```

This code was compiled and uploaded on to the Arduino Board. Then it was tested successfully on the motors. Screenshot of code is given in Fig. 9.3

KIDS_Bluetooth_HC06 | Arduino 1.8.2

File Edit Sketch Tools Help

KIDS_Bluetooth_HC06 §

```
#include <SoftwareSerial.h>
SoftwareSerial BlueTooth(2, 3);    // (TXD, RXD) of HM-10
char BT_input;          // to store input character received via BT.
int motorPin1 = 7;      // pin 7 on L293D IC
int motorPin2 = 5;      // pin 5 on L293D IC
int motorPin3 = 9;     // pin 9 on L293D IC
int motorPin4 = 11;     // pin 11 on L293D IC

void setup()
{
  BlueTooth.begin(9600);
  Serial.begin(9600);
pinMode(motorPin1, OUTPUT);
pinMode(motorPin2, OUTPUT);
pinMode(motorPin3, OUTPUT);
pinMode(motorPin4, OUTPUT);
}

void loop()
{
  if (BlueTooth.available())
  {
BT_input=BlueTooth.read();
    if (BT_input=='s')
    {
```

Contd...

```
  {
BT_input=BlueTooth.read();
    if (BT_input=='s')
    {
digitalWrite(motorPin1, LOW);
digitalWrite(motorPin2, LOW);
digitalWrite(motorPin3, LOW);
digitalWrite(motorPin4, LOW);
Serial.println("Motors are Off");
    }
    else if (BT_input=='b')
    {
digitalWrite(motorPin1, LOW);
digitalWrite(motorPin2, HIGH);
digitalWrite(motorPin3, LOW);
digitalWrite(motorPin4, HIGH);
Serial.println("Motors are rotating left");
    }
    else if (BT_input=='f')
    {
digitalWrite(motorPin1, HIGH);
digitalWrite(motorPin2, LOW);
digitalWrite(motorPin3, HIGH);
digitalWrite(motorPin4, LOW);
Serial.println("Motors are rotating right");
    }
   else if (BT_input=='r')
    {

digitalWrite(motorPin1, HIGH);
digitalWrite(motorPin2, LOW);
digitalWrite(motorPin3, HIGH);
digitalWrite(motorPin4, LOW);
Serial.println("Motors are rotating right");
    }
   else if (BT_input=='r')
    {
digitalWrite(motorPin1, HIGH);
digitalWrite(motorPin2, LOW);
digitalWrite(motorPin3, LOW);
digitalWrite(motorPin4, HIGH);
Serial.println("First Motor is rotating right & Second is left");
    }
    else if (BT_input=='l')
    {
digitalWrite(motorPin1, LOW);
digitalWrite(motorPin2, HIGH);
digitalWrite(motorPin3, HIGH);
digitalWrite(motorPin4, LOW);
Serial.println("First Motor is rotating Left & second is right");
    }
  }
}
```

Fig. 9.3: Screenshot of controlling motors from mobile phone via Bluetooth.

Additional Commands of Bluetooth

1. #include <SoftwareSerial.h> : Includes app named SoftwareSerial.h
2. SoftwareSerialBluetooth(2,3); : Does not transmit but only receives data
3. char BT_input; :Character received via BT is taken as input
4. Bluetooth.begin(9600) : Data transmission rate between Bluetooth and mobile is set at 9600 bauds
5. If Bluetooth.available()){
   BT_input=Bluetooth.read();
   if (BT_input=='<variable stored on mobile say forward>')
   { < write 4 statements for 2 motors to go forward> }
       else if (BT_input=='variable stored on mobile say backward>')
   { < write 4 statements for 2 motors to go forward> }
       else if(BT_input=='< similar to above]
       else if <similar to above>}

Let's Have More Fun

Use of both the Bluetooth modules HM-10 and HC-06.

Study both the Bluetooth modules HM-10 and HC-06. Write code for each of these and see the difference.

Chapter 10

SENSING AN OBSTACLE AND WARNING THE CAR DRIVER

(USE OF IR AND ULTRASONIC SENSORS)

Need

On long monotonous drives, automobile drivers tend to feel drowsy. If, at that time, an obstacle comes in front, the vehicle is likely to collide with it resulting in potential loss of life and damage to the vehicle itself.

However, if there were an automatic system to sense an obstacle and raise an alarm or stop the car, it would have huge road safety applications. Isn't it?

What will we learn?

In this project, we'll learn the following:

- Ultrasonic Obstacle Sensor
- Functioning of Ultrasonic sensor
- Coding to sense an obstacle and raise alarm

Principle of Obstacle Sensors?

To sense an obstacle, a transmitter is used to transmit a wave/pulse. This wave/pulse could be in the infra-red (IR) frequency range or ultrasonic frequency range. If an obstacle is in the line of the wave, the wave gets reflected and is received by a receiver. Total time taken by the transmitted wave to get reflected and reach the receiver gives an indication of the distance of the obstacle.

Hence, obviously, this type of sensor module has a pair of devices namely a transmitter and a receiver.

Normally there are two types of sensors used for this purpose. One is IR (infrared) sensor and the second is ultrasonic sensor. Details of IR sensor have been covered in the previous chapters. In this chapter details of Ultrasonic Sensor will be covered.

What is an Ultrasonic Sensor?

An ultrasonic sensor module is a device which transmits sound waves at a frequency too high for humans to hear (hence the word *'Ultra'-sonic*). When some object comes in the path of these waves, they get reflected back. Distance of the object is calculated based on the time taken by the reflected ultrasonic wave to reach the receiver after reflecting off the obstacle.

In this project, we used a sensor named HC-SRO4 which is similar to SRF 05 shown in Fig. 10.1. This sensor can determine the distance of the object comfortably up to 12 feet.

Fig 10.1: Ultrasonic Sensor

These sensors can be fitted in cars to sound an alert if an some obstacle comes in front. Also, these give an idea of the distance of the obstacle from the car so that due precautionary action could be taken to avoid collision. Stretching the same line of imagination a little further, these sensors may activate the car brakes if the obstacle is closer than a pre-determined distance. However, like before; let us not get too ahead of ourselves!

Pins in Ultrasonic Sensor Module

The ultrasonic sensor has 4/5 pins. Two pins, Vcc and Gnd, are needed to give power supply to the module for its functioning. Power is taken from the Arduino board from its pins 5 V DC and GND.

The third pin, Trig, is used for sending ultrasonic wave and the pin, Echo, is used to receive the reflected wave.

Connection with Arduino

Connections of various pins of ultrasonic sensor module with Arduino board are shown in Fig. 10.2.

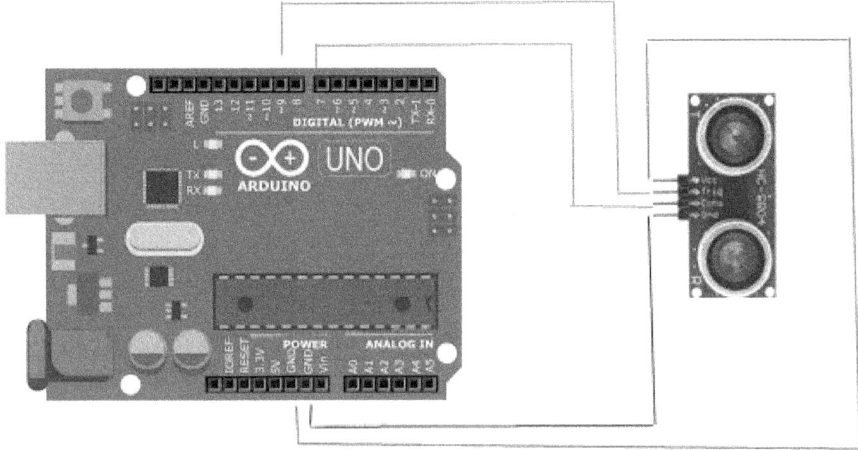

Fig 10.2: Connection of Ultrasonic Sensor with Arduino Board

Code to Measure Distance of the Obstacle

Let us first define the pin numbers of Arduino board where we get sensor's output.

```
    #define trig 10
    #define echo 8
        // this constant won't change.  It's the pin number of the
sensor's output:
  void setup() {
Serial.begin (9600);      // Setting data transfer rate as 9600
bauds
pinMode(trig, OUTPUT);
pinMode(echo, INPUT);
  }
   void loop() {
      float duration, distance;
digitalWrite(trig, LOW);
delayMicroseconds(2);
digitalWrite(trig, HIGH);
delayMicroseconds(10);
digitalWrite(trig, LOW);
       duration = pulseIn(echo, HIGH);
       distance = duration / 58;
Serial.print(distance);
Serial.println("cm");
delay(1000);
  }
```

With this code, we can note the distance of the object from the sensor.

Let's Have More Fun

Write code to sound buzzer when the distance of the obstacle is less than 10 feet from the moving car.

Chapter 11

ARDUINO HARDWARE BASICS & COMMON HARDWARE DEVICES

General

Arduino Board is a small, palm sized hardware circuit, which can be programmed and used to perform a variety of functions. It was designed by engineering students in Italy during 2005, as part of their project. The aim was to make a device that could connect many things like fan, bulbs, motors, various sensors etc. and produce solutions to day-to-day problems.

To use this board, they made a software called Arduino IDE (Integrated Development Environment). This IDE can be downloaded from the internet. It helps one to write computer code for any project/problem and upload it from the desktop computer to the Arduino Board.

Suggested Projects

1. To switch on a fan or AC automatically when it becomes hot e.g., temperature >30^{0}C
2. To switch on the street light automatically when it becomes dark and switch it off when day breaks.
3. To automatically sprinkle water on the indoor and outdoor plants when the soil becomes dry.
4. To raise an alarm when the house is locked, and some undesirable person tries to enter it.
5. To make a moving car robot and control it using a mobile phone.

Arduino Board

1. Key Features of Arduino Board

a. It can read inputs from sensors like temperature sensor, light detecting sensor, motion detector sensor, moisture sensor and, based on the code written, switch on a fan, light, air-conditioner, sprinkler or drive motors etc.

b. It can read both digital as well as analog signals from any sensor and give output to switch on any device.

c. Its programming language is easy and a simplified version of C++ language.

d. It has a small computer in the form of an Integrated Circuit (IC) which is called Microcontroller. It is the brain of a computer and performs all functions. It is made by ATMEL company. Microcontroller used in Arduino UNO is ATmega328P.

e. There are many types of Arduino boards like Arduino Nano, Arduino Uno, Arduino Mini, Arduino Mega etc. Each board has different capabilities.

2. Hardware Components on the Board

Various components fitted on the Arduino UNO board are as shown in Fig. 11.1.

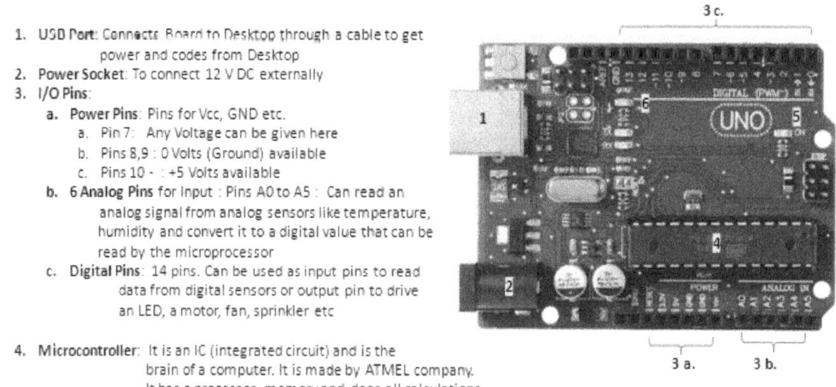

Fig 11.1: Components on Arduino Board

3. Connections on the Board

To use Arduino board, we need a computer/PC and a USB cable to connect it with the board as shown in Fig.11.2. Requirement of computer is:

- To download the Arduino software from the internet
- To write the code (Program) for any activity/project.
- To compile the code using Arduino software so that it is understood by the Arduino board.
- And finally, once code is proven on the computer, transfer (Upload) it from computer to the Arduino board.

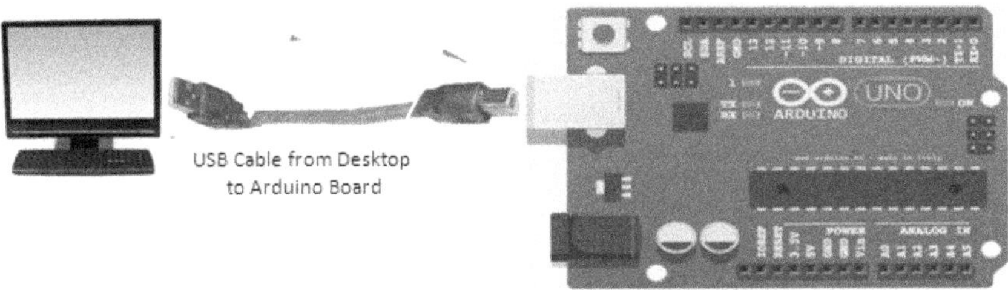

Fig 11.2: Connection between Desktop and Arduino Board

Other Hardware Components

1. LED

The full form of LED is Light Emitting Diode. It is a device which glows when electric current is passed through it. It has two terminals called anode and cathode. (Refer Fig. 11.3(a).)

In our circuits, we have used a small LED with a length of just around one centimeter. To light it, its anode terminal is connected to +5 Volts end of a battery or cell, and 0 V to its cathode.

2. Resistor

A resistor is a passive electrical component that restricts the flow of electric current in the electric circuits. In circuits using Arduino boards, it is generally used to restrict current in an LED or other components.

Pins of Arduino board provide up to 40 milliamperes of current, whereas an LED can take only up to 15 milliamperes of current. If more current is given to it, it gets overheated and burns. So, we connect a resistor in the circuit to restrict the current to 15 milliamperes.

Its unit of measurement is ohms (Ω) and its value is determined from the combination of colours on its circumference. Refer Fig. 11.6(a).

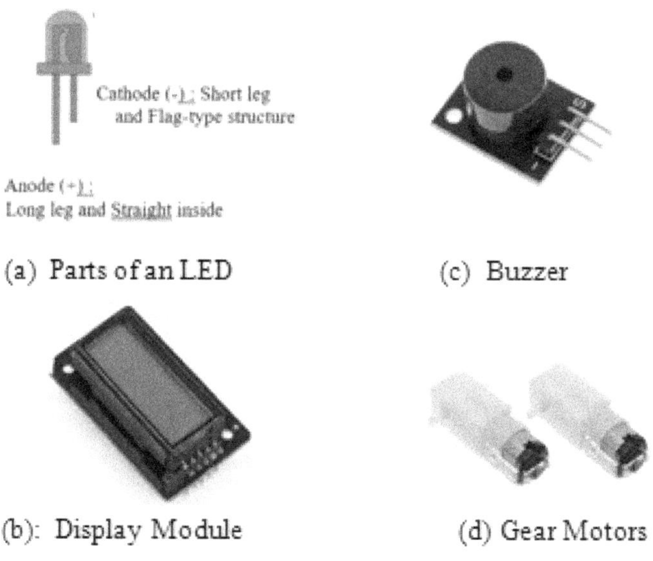

(a) Parts of an LED

(c) Buzzer

(b): Display Module

(d) Gear Motors

Fig 11.3: Hardware Components - Output Devices

3. Buzzer

A buzzer is a small component, which when connected to 5 V and GND of Arduino, generates tones (Fig. 11.3(c)). Frequency of tones can be changed by writing value of frequency in code.

One leg of the buzzer is connected to 5V of Arduino board and second leg to GND. Third pin of the buzzer is connected to a pin which is declared as OUTPUT pin.

4. LCD Modules or Display Module

LCD stands for Liquid Crystal Display. It is a small device on which any information can be displayed. We generally use it to see the data information sent by various sensors like temperature, humidity, resistance etc. to the Arduino board.

It has various types. Generally, 16x2 LCD is popular (refer Fig. 11.3 (b)) On this display, information can be displayed in 2 lines with each line having a maximum of 16 letters. If the information is longer, it can scroll also to right or left.

5. Gear Motors:

Motors are used to run wings of fans, wheels of cars and other appliances. The speed of the motors is generally very high as can be seen in the ceiling fans in our houses. However, for toy cars or the projects that students make in schools, we need motors which run at slow speeds. For that purpose, gear-motors are used.

6. Current Drivers

Gear motors generally take high current, maybe 100 milliamperes or so, for their operation. But the pins on the Arduino board supply only up to 40 milliamperes. So, to boost up current some current drivers are used. Gear motors are depicted in Fig. 11.3(d).

The common current driver is named LN293D. It has the capacity to run two gear motors at one time and give up to 2 amperes of current, which is sufficient for their operation.

Pin Connection Diagram:

The current driver LN293D is an integrated circuit (IC) based device with 16 pins (Fig. 11.4). Pins on the left side are from 1 to 8 and are used for running the first motor. On the right side, we have pin numbers 9 to 16 which are used to run the second motor. Pin layout is shown in Fig. 11.4. These are connected to Arduino as under:

- Pin 8 – It is Vs pin and is connected to Vc of Arduino where 5V DC is always available. The current driver gets 5 V at this pin from Arduino.
- Pins 4,5, 12 and 13 – These are Ground pins (GND) and are connected to GND of Arduino (means 0 volts).
- Pin 1 – ENABLE 1- When this pin gets 5 V, it enables all pins for Motor 1. So, to start Motor 1, this pin should be given 5V (or made HIGH)

- Pins 2 and 7: These are INPUT 1 pins and driver get inputs (5V or 0V called HIGH or LOW respectively) from Arduino based on the code.
- Pins 3 & 6: These are OUTPUT pins. Once the Driver gets inputs at pins 2 & 7, it amplifies the current and makes these available at pins 3 & 6 to which motors are connected.

Similarly, there are pins 9,10,11,14, 15 and 16 for Motor 2.

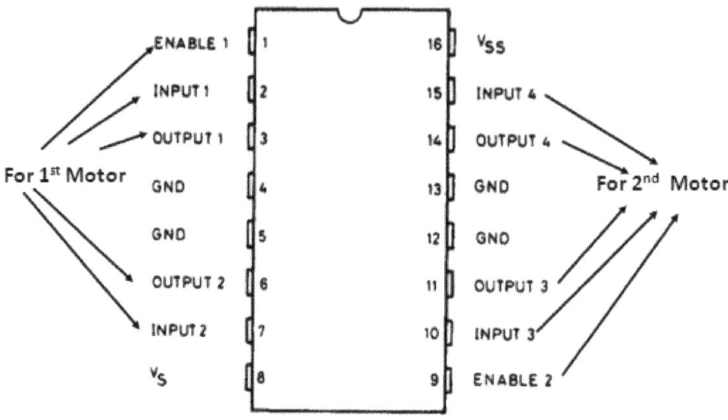

Fig 11.4: Pin Connections of IC LN293 D (Current Driver)

7. LDRs and LDR Module

The full form of LDR is Light Dependent Resistor. It is a small resistor, the value of which keeps changing with the intensity of light. A typical LDR has a resistance of 1000 ohms during night time and 50 ohms when it is kept in full day light.

It is very small in size, maybe 1 cm or so, and has 2 terminals as shown in Fig. 11.5(a).

LDRs are used as light sensors. These are also used in series with a resistor to make them functional in an Arduino circuit.

A better version of LDR, an LDR Module, shown in Fig. 11.5(b), is compatible with Arduino board. It is a small board with 4 pins and its performance is better than a simple LDR. Two of its pins are given power supply from the Arduino board and the value of resistance is read on the other two pins.

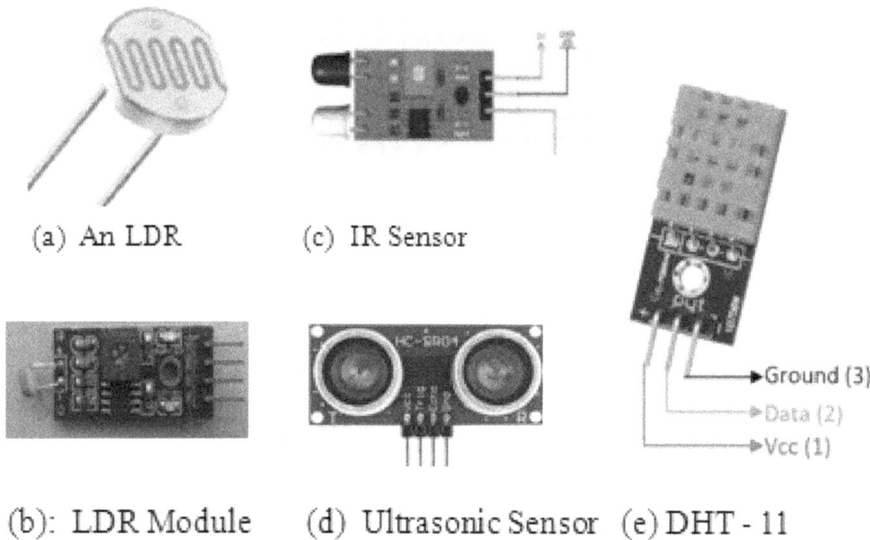

Fig 11.5: Hardware Components - Sensors

8. IR Sensors

IR stands for Infra-Red wave. This wave, once transmitted in air, moves in a straight line and gets reflected when some obstacle comes in front of it. It is used in ascertaining proximity of an object.

IR Proximity Sensor, used in Arduino circuit, has got two LEDs. One LED acts as a transmitter and the second one as a receiver (Fig. 11.5(c).

When switched on, Transmitter LED transmits IR wave. If some obstacle comes in front of it, the IR wave gets reflected and received by the Receiver LED, thus indicating presence of an object in front of it.

IR Sensor module has 3 pins. Two pins are connected to 5V and GND of Arduino whereas the third pin is a Data pin on which signal or 5V is received once an obstacle is noticed enroute.

9. Ultrasonic Sensors

An ultrasonic sensor module is a device which transmits sound waves at a frequency too high for humans to hear. Then they wait for the sound wave to get reflected, as and when some object comes in front of these waves. Distance of the object is calculated based on the time taken by the reflected sound wave after hitting the obstacle.

In the project, we used a sensor named HC-SRO4 and is shown in Fig. 11.5(d). This sensor can determine the distance of the object comfortably up to 12 feet.

These sensors can be fitted in cars or robots to know the presence of some obstacle in front of them. Also, these give an idea of the distance of the obstacle from the car so that due precautionary action could be taken to avoid collision.

Pins in Ultrasonic Sensor Module

The ultrasonic sensor has 4 pins. Two pins, Vcc and Gnd, are needed to give power supply to the module for its functioning. Power is taken from the Arduino board from its pins 5 V DC and GND.

Third pin is, Trig, is used for sending ultrasonic wave and the pin, Echo, is used to receive the reflected wave.

10. Digital Humidity & Temperature Sensor (DHT)

DHT is a small device which measures temperature or heat of a body and also the moisture present in the environment. At home, we use a thermometer to measure our body temperature when we fall sick. However, the sensors which are compatible with Arduino, are DHT-11 and DHT-22 and these are manufactured by many companies.

DHT is an abbreviation of Digital Humidity and Temperature. So, this sensor measures both temperature and humidity and gives digital output.

What does DHT-11 look like?

It has 3 pins as shown in Fig. 11.5(e). Two pins are connected to the power supply i.e. 5V and 0V (GND) of Arduino Board. We get the value of temperature as well as humidity on the 3rd pin.

Which DHT-11 to be used?

In our testing, we used DHT-11, which is compatible with Arduino, and is manufactured by Adafruit Industries, a US based company. A software/app to use DHT with Arduino, is available in the *Library* which can be downloaded from the internet. Complete code of DHT-11 is also written in this library.

11. Relay

A relay is a device which takes 5 V DC as input and can connect any appliance to 230 V AC. One such relay is shown at Fig. 11.6(b).

Functioning of Relay Module

Relay module has 3 pins (A,B,C) on one side and three connections (NC, COM, NO) on the other side. This module is activated by giving 5 V and 0 V (GND) at its pins A and B from the Arduino Board. Third pin C gets input from the digital pin of the Arduino Board.

On the other side, one connection (COM) is connected to the 230 V AC. And the second connection (NC) is connected to the home appliance.

When we write a code to HIGH at its input pin C, an internal coil, inside the relay module, gets magnetized and makes the connection of COM (230 V AC) to the other connection NC. So, 230 V is extended to the bulb which is connected as shown in Fig. 11.6(b).

Functioning of Relay Module

Relay module has 3 pins (A,B,C) on one side and three connections (NC, COM, NO) on the other side. This module is activated by giving 5 V and 0 V (GND) at its pins A and B from the Arduino Board. Third pin C gets input from the digital pin of the Arduino Board.

On the other side, one connection (COM) is connected to the 230 V AC. And the second connection (NC) is connected to the home appliance.

When we write a code to HIGH at its input pin C, an internal coil, inside the relay module, gets magnetized and makes the connection of COM (230 V AC) to the other connection NC. So, 230 V is extended to the bulb or any other home appliance.

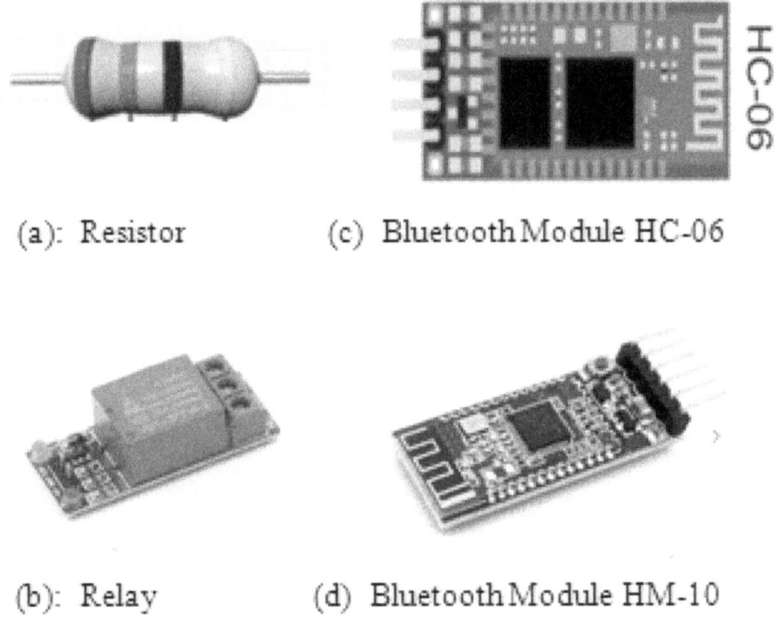

(a): Resistor (c) Bluetooth Module HC-06

(b): Relay (d) Bluetooth Module HM-10

Fig 11.6: Miscellaneous Hardware Components

12. Bluetooth Module

It is a small single-chip board, of the length less than 2 inches and breadth around 1 inch. It acts as a simple communication channel between a mobile phone and Arduino. Whatever commands we give from Mobile Phone, it understands and transmits to Arduino. This way, we can control any device remotely.

There are many types of Bluetooth modules based on the version of Bluetooth technology. Bluetooth modules based on version 2/2.1 are HC-06, HC-05 whereas the module based on later version 4.0 is HM-10.

Bluetooth Module HC-06

HC-05 and HC-06 are very popular and easy to interface. These are cheap and work at 3 mbps speed.

This module has 4 pins (two for power – Vcc and GND & 2 for Receive and Transmit data as shown in Fig. 11.6(c)). To use this, connect Vcc with 5V of Arduino and GND with GND of Arduino.

Rx and Tx pins are Receive and Transfer pins respectively. The module receives the serial data from the mobile phone through Rx pin and then transfers that data to the Arduino using its Tx pin.

The Tx pin on the module is connected directly to the Rx pin on the Arduino whereas the Rx pin on the module is connected to the Tx pin on the Arduino. Use of Tx pin of module also helps in generating 3.3V which is needed by the Bluetooth module. Connections of Arduino and Bluetooth Module pins are as shown in the Fig 9.2.

Bluetooth Module HM-10

This module (Fig. 11.6 (d)) is based on a later version of Bluetooth technology, namely, 4.0 version. It offers higher speed and higher range of operation, sometimes up to 100 meters. It works on 24 mbps speed.

Chapter 12

CODING FOR ARDUINO

Writing Code (Program)

Code written for Arduino is called **sketch.** Its basic structure has at most 3 parts which are explained in this chapter along with a few examples.

- **Basic Structure of Arduino Code:** Arduino Program has 3 parts (or 3 blocks) as under:
    - Block 1: Initial Statements (optional)
    - Block 2: Statements to be executed once
    - Block 3: Statements to be repeated again and again

- **Block I of the code**

  In the first block, some constants can be declared e.g., if an LED is permanently connected to Pin 9 of Arduino Board, it is written as:

  ```
  const int LED = 9
  ```

  i.e. the word 'LED' (also called a variable) will always be understood by Arduino as its pin 9. Also, as it is constant and integer, so the command is **const int** which is followed by the name given to the Pin of the Arduino board.

- **Block 2 of the Code:** This block is called **Set Up Block** and written as **void setup ( ).**

  (The originator of Arduino used the word **void** which means empty or hollow. He made Arduino for beginners whose knowledge is assumed to be hollow about problem solving).

Setup Block always starts with line **void setup()** followed by a few statements written with in curly brackets { }. It is the first function to be run in the program and is executed only once.

An example of Set Up Block is as under:

```
void setup()
   {
pinMode (9,OUTPUT);
pinMode (8, INPUT);
   }
```

There are two statements in the void set up block. The first statement pinMode (9, OUTPUT) will consider **Pin 9** of Arduino Board as always in **OUTPUT** mode. Items like an LED, a fan, an air conditioner, motor etc. can be connected to pin 9.

The second statement is **pinMode (8, INPUT**). With this statement, pin 8 of Arduino will always be considered as an **INPUT pin** and one can connect sensors like temperature sensor, light sensor, humidity sensors etc. to this pin.

- **Block 3 of the Code:** It is called **Loop Block** and written as **void loop()**. Here one can write those commands which are to be repeated again and again.

  Example is blinking of an LED which is to blink again and again, or a motor which is to run continuously. Code in this block is written as under:

```
void loop()   // keep repeating four statements below till end.
{
digitalWrite(13, HIGH); //It sends HIGH or +5 Volts to Pin No 13
 // to switch on a light or run a motor
delay(1000);  // pauses for 1,000 milli seconds i.e. one second
digitalWrite(13, LOW); // It sends LOW or 0 Volts to Pin No 13
 // So, it will switch off an LED
delay(1000);
}
```

As all the statements within the Loop Block will keep repeating, the LED connected to Pin13 will keep blinking with a gap of one second.

Points to Remember: First Line in the Code

1. After initial statements, the first line is always written as void setup();
2. This is followed by a start curly bracket {. Now, one can write code statements after it.
3. After writing all the statements, one must insert a closing curly bracket }.
4. Each statement is separated by a semi-colon (;).

Useful Commands and Instructions in Arduino Software

1. **Methods to Write Comments:** We should keep writing descriptions/ comments after each command so that we understand the code ourselves when we look at it at a later stage. The two ways of writing comments are shown below.

   a. **Line Statement**: If comment is short and can be fitted in one line then it can be written after two slashes //. So, anything written after two slashes is neither compiled, nor shown in the output. It is only to have a better understanding of the code.

```
Example: // This statement nominates Pin No. 13 as an Output Pin
```

   b. **Multiple-line Statements**: If the statement to be written is longer, then it can be written as /* ......multiple-statements */. Example

```
/* If an LED is connected to Pin No. 13, it will glow for 1
second, then remain off for next second and so on, so it will
keep blinking */
```

2. **Variables:** It is a way of naming or storing a numerical value for later use in the code. Example:

```
int RedLED = 13     /*Variable named RedLED is an integer and
given value 13. In the code, whenever the word 'RedLED' is
encountered, it will always be taken as 13.
```

3. **Constants:** The constants **HIGH and LOW** define the level at any pin. HIGH means +5Volts and LOW means 0 Volt. Example:

```
digitalWrite (13, HIGH);   // Arduino will send +5 Volts to
pin No. 13.
```

4. **Defining Mode of a Pin:** Any digital pin can be configured as an Input or Output pin using function pinMode. Example:

```
pinMode (13,OUTPUT);   // Pin No. 13 is configured as an
OUTPUT pin always.
```

5. **Reading from a Pin or Writing on to it:** There are four functions used to read from a pin or write on to it. These are:

```
a.  digitalRead (13);   // Reads status of pin No. 13 whether
    HIGH or LOW
b.  digitalWrite (13, HIGH);  //  Sends +5 Volts to pin No. 13
c.  analogRead (A0);  // Reads analog value from Analog Pin A0.
d.  analogWrite (A0, value);   // Sends the contents of
    variable 'value' to pin A0.
```

6. **Pausing code for a few seconds:** Command 'delay (milliseconds)' will pause the program for a few milliseconds. Example:

```
delay(1000);  // Pauses the code for 1000 milliseconds i.e one
second
```

7. **Serial Commands:**

   a. **Serial.begin(rate):** This command opens the serial port and sets baud rate for transmission of data from computer to Arduino board and backward. Generally, in most electronic equipment, baud rate of 9,600 is commonly used. Baud rate means number of bits per second.

Example:

```
Serial.begin(9600);     // Opens serial port and sets data
                           transmission rate as
                        //  9600 bits per second
```

a. **Serialprintln(data):** Prints data to the serial port in one line and goes to the start of next line. Example:

```
Serial.printlnanalogRead(0);  // Prints analog value on the monitor
```

Deleting the running code from Arduino memory

The memory of Arduino can store only one code at a time. Suppose you are running a code for, say, 'Blinking an LED' and want to write another code, then delete this code from the memory otherwise the existing code will keep running thus blinking of the LED will continue and disturb you. This is done as under:

click File,

click New,

click icons of Compile and Upload

As the NEW code is blank, so the 'Blinking of LED' will stop.

Some more commands and their meanings

Some common commands which are useful for writing common codes are tabulated below.

1. **Data Type is of Numerical Value**

   a. For small integer number up to 255

      byte *variable* = 50

   b. For large integer numbers up to 2^{15} (from +32,767 to -32,767)

      int *variable* = 40000

c. For very large integer numbers

long *variable* = 50000

d. For decimal number

float *variable* = 8.9

2. **Arithmetic Operations**

Most of the arithmetic symbols can be used in coding. Examples are:

```
Addition     +,          Example:        a = b+c
Subtraction   -,                         a = b-c
Multiplication   *,                      a = b*c
Division            /,                   a = b/c
For increment by 1    ++,                // Equivalent to a = a+1
For decrement by 1    - -,               // Equivalent to a = a-1
```

3. **Conditional Statements**

```
If (condition)
    {execute these statements and go to next line};

Example is:
 if (Light < 250)
    {digitalWrite(LED, HIGH}

There is another way of writing conditional statements known as
if(..) [..]; else {..};

Example is:
 if (Light < 250)
    {digitalWrite(LED, HIGH};
 else {digitalWrite(LED, LOW};
```

That way there are many more commands and one is recommended to use the authorized manual of Arduino Company for their correct use. Even the commands listed above should be used after consulting the authorized manual of the company.

CONCLUSION

In this book, a sincere effort has been made to collate and pass on the information which we got while studying and interacting with our seniors. We are told that Arduino board was earlier taught to the students at technical colleges. However, now it has percolated down to the school level too.

The Govt. of India has made an effort to educate students by supplying them kits in the Atal Tinkering Labs. However, the ground reality is that these kits are not available in most of the schools. In some schools, where the kits are available, the teachers themselves are not conversant with their use and as a result, these kits rarely see the light of day from their confines of the laboratory cupboards!

After doing a bit of reading and interacting with a few technically qualified people, we realised that school students can also use Arduino and learn coding. By doing this, they can come up with really cool projects, take on some of the problems/issues bugging the class or prevalent in the environment and use their Arduino knowledge to solve these.

We are certain that school students will definitely derive some inspiration and a lot of benefit from this book! Happy coding!

www.ingramcontent.com/pod-product-compliance
Ingram Content Group UK Ltd.
Pitfield, Milton Keynes, MK11 3LW, UK
UKHW062258290726
14090UKWH00017B/758